Coming Clean

Dirty Little Secrets from a Professional Housecleaner

by

Schar Ward

Book Peddlers
Minnetonka, MN

cover design: Mighty Media, Minneapolis, MN
cover squeegee: Casabella, Blauvelt, NY

ISBN 0-916773-87-6
UPC 607966 87602

copyright@ 2002 Schar Ward
first printing, March 2002

Publisher's Cataloging-in-Publication
(Provided by Quality Books, Inc.)
Ward, Schar.
   Coming clean : dirty little secrets from a
professional housecleaner / by Schar Ward. --1st ed.
   p. cm.
   Includes bibliographical references and index.
   ISBN: 0-916773-87-6

   1. House cleaning.   I. Title.
TX324.W37 2002   648".5
                    QB101-201284

BOOK PEDDLERS
15245 Minnetonka Blvd, Minnetonka, MN 55345
952-912-0036 • fax 952-912-0105
www.bookpeddlers.com

printed in the USA

02   03   04   05   06   07   08   09   10 9 8 7 6 5 4 3 2

Table of Contents

acknowledgements

My most sincere and heartfelt thanks to my long-time dear friend and former business partner, Joyce Gaydosik, for her help in writing the original book, her never-ending support and encouragement, and her love and friendship throughout the past thirty years.

Thanks to my children Debra, Bob and Betty Jo for believing in their mom and never letting me forget how to laugh, or what really counts.

I thank my mom for teaching me to "either do it right or don't do it at all," and my dad for his wonderful Missouri humor. Thanks to Aunt Betty for her interest and caring when it would have been a whole lot easier not to.

My thanks to the thousands of seminar participants who listened, shared with me, and allowed me to impact their homes and lives.

And to my publisher, Vicki Lansky, at Book Peddlers for believing in and being excited about this project. I thank her and her staff, especially Jean Borgen, who, besides undangling my participles and organizing my stream of consciousness, contributed her style and own wonderful sense of humor to the book.

introduction

This is a book about work simplification in your home. It has to do with chasing dust and dirt. The books give you a step-by-step approach to daily, weekly, monthly and spring and fall cleaning. It tells you what supplies and equipment you need, and how to use them. It teaches you where to store things and how. It helps you get organized.

I am one of the founders of Domestic Engineering, Inc. (est. 1970). My first business partner, Joyce Gaydosik, and I worked side-by-side cleaning and giving seminars for almost twenty years. Today my business/seminar partner is my daughter, Debra Varin. My alter ego, *Clara Klutz*, has made these seminars a joyful adventure.

During the years of owning a cleaning service I have been ridiculed, praised, yelled at, laughed at, propositioned, looked down on, looked up to and seen some sights you would not believe!

My hope is that **COMING CLEAN** makes your life easier and tidier. Beyond that, it's to let you know you're not the only one who's hidden dirty dishes in the oven only to forget and preheat them a few days later.

Schar Ward

A Note of Caution

Care and caution are important when using the information in this book. Conditions and situations are unique to each of us. Products should be tested in inconspicuous areas first. Always follow information on product labels. Common sense counts. Schar Ward and Book Peddlers disclaim any liability from the use or misuse of any product or idea presented in this book.

Chapter 1

Unleash Your Inner Cleaning Woman

Domestic Engineering services several hundred homes each month. It requires some complicated scheduling that usually works for everyone involved, but sometimes it gets away from us.

An older couple called early one Wednesday morning to cancel. Seems they weren't feeling well. When the cancellation came in, we also found a scheduling error. Two sets of workers were scheduled for that same job.

In vain, we tried to reach all the cleaning people involved. Next best, we tried to get to the address before our workers arrived. Hopefully, we could intercept our staff before they disturbed the ailing seniors. There were no cars in front of the residence. We hoped that meant neither of our two crews had shown up yet. Our hopes faded the longer we waited.

Then from the curb, we saw the husband toss open the front door, throw up his arms and shout back into the house, "Good grief, here come two more!" We imagine he still relates being ill with being bombarded by cleaning women.

The Importance of Your Home

Have you ever thought seriously about how important the condition of your home is to your family?

Your home should be a place where your family can retreat from the world. Your home should be a place your family looks forward to coming to, not coming from! It's a place to relax, be comforted and renew your strength.

A clean home reduces stress, since a mess is depressing. All of life's problems seem larger when your home is "out of control." But if the house is neat and clean, other stresses become easier to handle.

Your home is where your children learn right from wrong, patience, love and regard for family and others. What you teach them in your home today is shaping the way they will teach their children tomorrow.

The home is where it all begins and has for generations. The schools used to share the burden of teaching some virtues, but because of overcrowding and other factors, they can't any longer. It's your job as a parent to keep a clean home and to teach your children the importance of cleanliness.

People give all sorts of excuses for not cleaning their homes. I'll answer as many arguments as I can think of.

"I can't (or won't) keep a clean house because…"
1) "I will not be a slave to my house."
The surest way to become a slave to anything is to not be in control of it.

2) "The dirt will be there when I get back."
That's true, only it doesn't just wait—it multiplies.

3) "My house can look lived in."
Do you also want your bed to look slept in and your clothes to look wellworn?

4) "I won't live by a schedule or routine."
Freedom without bounds leads to a jungle.

5) "I don't have time."
Time is like money—you don't find it, you make it.

6) "It doesn't tax my intelligence."
Neither does eating, but you haven't given that up.

7) "Life is short; we should stop and smell the flowers."
Flowers are much easier to find in a well-maintained garden.

8) "I hate housework."
Attitude begins with thought. Change your attitude! Give thanks for all those material possessions you're so lucky to have.

Attitude

The right attitude is the first thing we try to teach new employees.

You may be asking, "How can I have a good attitude about doing something I dislike?" You have to rearrange your thinking about housework. If you have the right equipment, supplies and this book, you can clean your home without it being a big chore. Approach cleaning like you would any other job. It takes practice and preparedness to do a good job.

Coming Clean

Cleanliness is contagious. As a professional housecleaner, I see examples all the time of households that have gone from health hazards to *House Beautiful*. I've gone into homes where the family was on the verge of moving just to get away from the mess. After I got their home in shape for them, they took pride in their surroundings, and they helped keep it clean.

Appearance

The next step is proper appearance. As an employer of cleaning professionals, I establish guidelines on the appearance of employees. But your appearance matters, too.

The way you look influences the way you work. Not to suggest dressing in heels and a long dress to clean house, especially if you're a man. But being dressed neatly and comfortably lends itself to getting the work done.

If you set aside part of Saturday to clean, put on your make-up and do your hair first. Or for men—shave and put on a clean T-shirt. You'll feel and look presentable if visitors drop by. It'll also keep you from thinking "How awful I look!" every time you clean a mirror.

Wear tennis shoes while housecleaning. They're comfortable, and they help prevent slipping if you climb step stools or ladders. A pair of loose slacks and a white blouse or T-shirt completes your outfit. "Why a white blouse/T-shirt?" It seems that wearing a white top just does something to make you feel more like cleaning. Try it and see!

Lean 'n Clean Exercises

You can get your home and yourself into shape at the same time. Stretch as you shine, hop when you mop and wiggle while you wax. Play some mood music in the background—whatever gets you moving.

Open your windows and let as much fresh air in the room as weather permits.

Lean 'n Clean exercises are scattered throughout the book. They're in the cleaning sections where you'll most likely use them. They won't appeal to everyone, but if you try it, you might like it. They're quick and easy. Check page 114 for a complete listing of the exercises.

Your Cleaning Profile

Housekeeping can provide insights into your nature, aptitudes, strengths and weaknesses. For example, if you're the type who'll use any excuse to take a break, put your feet up right now and take this quiz.

Identify the description that best reflects your habits and note your answers.

1) Do you make your bed. . .
    a. As soon as you get up?
    b. An hour or two later?
    c. Just close the door and forget it!

Coming Clean

2) Do you take your clothes out of the dryer. . .
   a. Before the buzzer stops?
   b. Before the clothes are cool?
   c. Two days later and throw them in a basket?

3) Do you wipe up spills. . .
   a. Before they hit the ground?
   b. Before it hardens?
   c. By scraping them off the floor?

4) Do you mend clothing. . .
   a. Instantly?
   b. When you can?
   c. When monkeys fly?

5) If guests spill ashes on your carpet, do you. . .
   a. Vac underneath their feet?
   b. Pick up the worst and wait until they leave?
   c. Say, "don't worry about it" and spill your own to make
      your guests more comfortable?

6) When your husband invites the boss for dinner, do you. . .
   a. Get out the Julia Child's cookbook and clean the house?
   b. Light a few candles and set an extra plate?
   c. Call a marriage counselor?

7) Do you vacuum your carpeting. . .
   a. More often than you brush your teeth?
   b. Once a week and occasionally in-between?
   c. Before your mother-in-law comes for her bi-annual visit?

days with a receipt from any Barnes & Noble store.

Store Credit issued for new and unread books and unopened music after 30 days or without a sales receipt. Credit issued at <u>lowest sale price</u>.

We gladly accept returns of new and unread books and unopened music from bn.com with a bn.com receipt for store credit at the bn.com price.

Full refund issued for new and unread books and unopened music within 30 days with a receipt from any Barnes & Noble store.

Store Credit issued for new and unread books and unopened music after 30 days or without a sales receipt. Credit issued at <u>lowest sale price</u>.

We gladly accept returns of new and unread books and unopened music from bn.com with a bn.com receipt for store credit at the bn.com price.

Full refund issued for new and unread books and unopened music within 30 days with a receipt from any Barnes & Noble store.

Store Credit issued for new and unread books and unopened music after 30 days or without a sales receipt. Credit issued at <u>lowest sale price</u>.

We gladly accept returns of new and unread books and unopened music from

8) Do you clean your children's rooms. . .
    a. For them because they can't do it good enough?
    b. Once they have it picked up?
    c. No. They live in it, so who cares?

9) Do you rotate the cushions on your furniture. . .
    a. While guests are sitting on them?
    b. When you vacuum them once a month?
    c. Less often than you rotate your tires?

If you answered "A" to most of the questions, consider yourself in need of therapy. You, no doubt, make other people nervous. Try to relax a little more and enjoy life.

If you answered "B" to most of the questions, you're as close to "normal" as most of us get. You're organized and neat to the extent you feel you must be and have reached that happy medium between "fuss" and "dust"!

If you answered "C" to most of the questions, check to see if your shoelaces are tied. Get professional cleaning help, at least initially. You are most in need of this book but may only read the chapter titles and look at the pictures.

Professional Cleaning Services

This isn't an ad for cleaning services. But if you've reached the point where you don't know where to start, your smartest move may be to call a professional cleaning service. It'll give you a one-time, thorough cleaning. It's amazing what that boost can do for you.

If you make the decision to hire professional cleaners for your home, here are some guidelines to help you get the most for your money:

- Select an established company. Ask around to find satisfied customers, or check the yellow pages. If it's been around for a few years and still has the original owners, it's got a track record.

- Does the cleaning company train its employees? Ask about the training program.

- The management should ask to interview you—in your home—as a matter of routine. Companies that don't bother with home interviews aren't too concerned with their employees, or with your needs.

- Find out who furnishes supplies and equipment—you or the cleaners. If you're fussy about cleaning products, you'll want to provide your own.

- What kind of insurance does the company carry? They may or may not be bonded and insured for loss or damage. (Still, insurance coverage is less important than integrity and reliability.)

- Make sure the cleaning company pays Social Security, state and federal taxes. If the service is not doing the withholding, the IRS considers the homeowner, as employer, liable for payment.

- Ask to see references. Get phone numbers of several current and past clients, and call them.

Instead of a service, you might find a person who enjoys cleaning, and does it for a living. Make sure it's a reliable and responsible person.

Keep in mind most cleaning services do not strip floors, shampoo carpets, do laundry, or wash whole walls or ceilings.

And don't forget to pay the required taxes and withholding for anyone working in your home.

Chapter 2

𝒯-i-d-y is a
𝒻our-ℒetter 𝒲ord

Many Domestic Engineering clients trust us with their house keys. One autumn day Maria and Ellie tried to get a key to work in the back door of a client's home. The key turned, but the door wouldn't open. Ellie tried the key while Maria pushed. Maria tried the key while Ellie pushed. A neighbor woman watched both of them from her kitchen window.

Maria and Ellie circled the house trying doors and windows. They regrouped at the back door and attacked again with steely determination. They didn't stop working on the lock until a male voice asked, "What's going on here?" They turned around to face two policemen with drawn guns.

Maria immediately forgot all the English she ever knew. That didn't stop her from loudly explaining, in Spanish and pantomime, that they were merely trying to break into this home. Ellie managed to give an officer a business card.

Since a neighbor had reported a possible burglary, and Maria was doing her best to confess, the women were loaded into the back of the squad car. Maria has since added to her English vocabulary, "I'm innocent—I work here."

Get Rid Of It

Some people pride themselves on being real "savers." They're the same people who complain they can't keep up with their cleaning. If you're a busy person, and who isn't?, it doesn't make sense to keep a lot of things around to dust. Some people move to bigger houses because they "need" more room, when all they really need is fewer belongings.

Most people have more "collectibles" in their house than they can afford to store. I can tell you from experience that cleaning is much easier and faster if you keep bric-a-brac and clutter to a minimum. Things that have to be lifted, cleaned, washed or dusted, cleaned under and then replaced, all add to the total cleaning time. To keep a clean house and save time, get rid of everything you don't need!

Just pretend you are going to move to another house or an apartment. As you are going through your things, ask yourself these three questions:

- Can anyone in my family use this?
- How frequently will we use it?
- If I keep it, how will I store it?

Do your de-junking on the day, or the day before, your trash is picked up. Why? Because there will be less time for your family to drag stuff back in the house. Do one room at a time so you aren't overwhelmed.

Get four boxes. Label them:
- Charity
- Junk
- Recycle
- Sort

Use the three questions above to help you decide which items to keep. In the box marked "Sort," put things you think you might need. Seal the Sort box and store it somewhere out of the way. In a year, if you haven't needed to open the box, toss it.

That routine, followed twice a year, goes a long way toward simplifying housework.

Where To Put What

After you've gotten rid of everything you don't need, your next step is to put things in their proper place. To decide where you should store items, ask yourself these questions:

- Where will I use it?
- How frequently will I use it?
- Where will I look for it?

Store items where they'll be used. The ones most often used should be in the most convenient places. If things are going to be used together, store them together. It helps, too, if you can teach your family to return things to their proper place.

"Where will I look for it?" is a great way to decide where to store seldom-used things.

Organize

If you work outside the home, you know that the way today's person-on-the-go is shown in magazines and TV ads is fiction.

According to the ads, if you use the right toothpaste or deodorant, you'll feel as fresh arriving home as when you left that morning. I don't care what type of mouthwash or soap you use— when evening comes around, you're tired and not so fresh. Yet your day has, no doubt, several hours to go. You may have the evening meal to prepare, laundry to do and the house to pick up. If you have children, you have to find time to be a parent, too. That's why organization is so important.

To List or Not to List

Most books about organization tell you to start by making all kinds of lists. If you work better with a list, fine. But if you don't, it's okay. A home is not a factory, *thank goodness!,* and it can't be organized the same way.

Personally, I don't like set schedules. Many people don't like organizing themselves because it involves self-discipline and thinking ahead. Yes, you have to learn to budget your time. Still, you don't need to be rigid. Keep it loose. Then you can scrap the plan, or change it, whenever it doesn't fit real life.

When you're organized, you're efficient. There's no job, whether bathing a baby or running a computer, that isn't easier, quicker and more enjoyable if you think about it logically, in advance.

A bit of consistency saves lots of time and energy. If you learn to do a few things every day, and when they need doing, you've discovered the secret of organization.

Decide on the level of cleanliness that suits you and your family. Then decide how many hours you can spend on house-cleaning. Don't be influenced by how clean your mother-in-law's house is kept, or that of Great-Aunt Agatha's. Remember, those women don't have the same obligations that you do. The comfort of your family is all that matters.

Set realistic goals for yourself. It's far better to do one or two "extra" things a day, rather than tackle it all at once.

Daily Schedule

If your house is neat, it'll appear clean. If the house is untidy, however, "clean" won't show. There should be a place for everything and everything should be in its place. (Organizing, room-by-room, is covered later.)

Dust Buster Strut

Make it a habit to walk briskly from room to room.

- Learn to do daily chores quickly and efficiently. Use every available means to make the job easier.

- Make the beds.

- Use comforters in place of bedspreads to save valuable time. Kids are more likely to make their own beds with comforters.

- Pick up dirty clothes. Each family member should pick up their own dirty clothes and put them in a hamper you have cleverly left in each bedroom.

- Wipe off the bathroom counter, sink, bowl and mirror for spots and spatters.

> Keep a bottle of spray disinfectant, window cleaner and paper towels in each bathroom for quick wipe-ups. Consider purchasing disinfecting wet wipes.

- Put away food and wipe off range and countertops.

- Pick up or straighten books and toys.

- Dust tabletops, if necessary.

> When dusting, use a clean, slightly moist cloth to cut down on friction and static electricity. Use a feather duster very lightly sprayed with room freshener if you're in a real hurry. (Feather dusters don't work when they're wet.)

- Sweep or vacuum high-traffic floor areas, as needed.

- Clean pet areas.

- Do the laundry as needed.

Daily cleaning and straightening should take a few minutes to a half hour, excluding laundry. But that really means <u>every</u> <u>day</u>, so things don't pile up.

Weekly Cleaning

If you clean once a week (or every two weeks, if your household is small and tidy), the time estimates used by Domestic Engineering are:

• Kitchen	45 minutes
• Living Room/Family Room	30 minutes
• Each Bathroom	30 minutes
• Each Bedroom	30 minutes

While the time spent room to room varies with each household, if you use the guidelines I've given as a target goal, soon you'll be cleaning like a professional.

Safety

Most accidents happen in the home, but with care, you can avoid them. No book on cleaning would be complete without a section on safety.

- Be careful how you mix and store cleaning chemicals. Many are caustic and dangerous.

> Never mix chlorine bleach with any other chemical. The mixing of bleach and ammonia, intentional or otherwise, creates a toxic gas. (Don't leave any bleach in a potty chair chamber. A child's urine contains ammonia and creates toxic gas.)

- Do open windows when using strong chemicals, especially in small areas like bathrooms.

- Use a dustpan and broom to pick up broken glass or anything broken. Follow up with a damp paper towel. Don't try to pick up glass with your bare hands.

- Keep sharp knives where no one can get hurt. Use a wooden holder on the counter, near the wall. Don't keep knives in a drawer where you might cut yourself reaching for other utensils. *(It also dulls the blades to be rubbing against other metals.)*

- Don't lift anything heavier than is comfortable for you. Ask for help if necessary.

- Don't wear blouses with kimono-type sleeves.

Coming Clean

- When using a stepladder, don't move it with anything perched on it. Make sure a ladder is firmly anchored before climbing. Never stand on the top step.

- Use a step stool to reach high places, not chairs.

- Don't place your bucket under a ladder. Have you ever stepped in a bucket of cleaning water?

- Keep a rag under your cleaning pail. A pinhole leak plus chlorine solution could spell disaster for a floor or carpet.

- Don't plug anything into over-utilized receptacles. You risk overloading a circuit.

- Remember, water and electricity don't mix. When using a mop, stay away from electrical cords.

- All electrical appliances should have a three-prong outlet to ground the device.

- Replace cracked or frayed appliance cords immediately.

- Dry your hands before plugging or unplugging appliances. When unplugging, pull the plug, not the cord.

- Always unplug small electrical appliances before cleaning them.

- Unless advertised as a wet/dry vac, don't use a vacuum cleaner for anything wet.

- Don't use a vacuum cleaner on outdoor carpet, even if it looks dry.

- Don't leave home with an appliance, such as a washing machine or dishwasher, still running. *(That could be the one time something breaks and causes a flood or fire.)*

- Always read and follow manufacturer's directions on cleaning products. If it says, "wear rubber gloves," wear them. If it says, "use sparingly," then do just that.

Keep your family safe while you get them tidied up and organized.

Chapter 3

Home in De-Range?
Kitchen Clean-Up

Domestic Engineering, my cleaning company, is based in Minnesota, land of 10,000 lakes and just as many blizzards.

Helen didn't drive during snowfalls, so I drove her to a client's home and gave her the house key. Our key wouldn't work in the front door lock. Mountains of snow surrounded the rest of the house.

We found shovels. We shoveled a path across the front of the house. We shoveled around the side of the house and, eventually, to the back patio door. The patio snowdrifts were lovely. They obviously hadn't been disturbed all winter. Just waiting for spring was beginning to seem like a good idea. But, we shoveled the patio.

When we gained full access to the patio door, we found a locked screen. I studied the screen until I found a hole big enough for a pencil to slide through. The pencil wiggling finally lifted the screen latch. The glass patio door was unlocked. Apparently a mountain of snow was the security system for that door.

Helen appreciated my efforts to help her get into the house. "Thank goodness that worked," she said, "now you won't have to stuff me down the chimney."

Kitchen

Getting your kitchen organized will make it easier to clean. Even when it's well organized, the kitchen usually takes longer to clean than any other room.

- Put the knife-holder next to the breadboard to save lots of steps.

- Store pots and pans near the stove. Hang them inside cupboard doors or the back of the broom closet door. Although pans hanging on a rack look very decorative, hanging them means keeping their bottoms shiny. Of course, that's more work.

- Don't put your spice racks next to the stove. Cooking heat dries spices and herbs. To make your spices easier to find, arrange them in alphabetical order.

- If you can afford the space, organize spices in a drawer.

Dish Pan Dishco

When washing dishes or countertops, use a circular motion with full arm. Reverse your motion after a few wipes. It helps tone your arms and strengthen your wrists.

- Canned goods should be stored in lower cupboards. Use slide-out or revolving shelves.

Coming Clean

- Store cans, bottles and boxes of long pasta in a wine rack for easy access.

- Glasses, dishes and silverware are best stored near the dishwasher and convenient to the table. If you must choose between the two, choose the dishwasher.

> Put a small sponge on the soap dish under the cake of soap. It keeps the soap firm, and the sponge is always handy for quick touch-up cleaning.

- Don't store your fine china in the same cupboard as your everyday stoneware. To prevent scratches on your fine china plates, place a paper napkin or a coffee filter between stacked dishes.

- See-through canisters are ideal for sugar, rice, etc. You can tell at a glance when you need to add them to your shopping list.

- Try to find canisters you can open using only one hand. The outsides stay cleaner.

- A good way to store bottle caps, extra baby-bottle caps, etc. is to glue or nail the metal tops of pint jars to the underside of a cabinet shelf. You can screw jars easily into place and everything is visible.

- Keep an old toothbrush on hand to clean around faucets, appliance knobs, food processors, etc.

- All those bottles and little containers under the sink (that always seem to be sitting in water) can make the under-kitchen-sink area look awful. Don't place things directly on the floor of that cupboard. It's a good place, again, to use a turn-table, or try a wire basket.

- Use a silverware caddy to hold sponges and scouring pads or various sized plastic bags.

- You can store paper bags or small towels on the inside of cupboard doors.

Kitchen Sinks

Most people don't pay attention to their kitchen sinks until the sinks start to look bad.

Porcelain sinks develop what I call "pot marks." The marks look like little black scratches and are caused from things (usually pots and pans) scraping the sink. Stainless steel sinks are notorious for water spots. And of course, they both get hard water stains around the base of the faucets, and coffee and tea stains. It's easy to prevent stains and hard water buildup. Rinse and dry your sink after each use. However, if you haven't been doing that, you can still correct the problems.

To remove hard water deposits from around the faucets, apply a little phosphoric acid (see page 86), let it sit, then scrub with a soft pad, rinse and dry.

To remove pot marks, scrub with baking soda or liquid cleanser until spots disappear. No harsh abrasives—unless you have Corian®. If so, scrub away! Cleanser doesn't hurt Corian®, and a little scrubbing is good for it.

The coffee and tea stains can be removed with a mild solution of bleach and water. Or you can use baking soda on the stains. Be sure to rinse well and dry.

To remove water spots from stainless steel sinks, clean the sink well with a soft cleanser or baking soda. Rinse and dry. To really impress any guests, spray with a bit of Liquid Gold® furniture polish (or any oil), and buff to a high shine.

I'm amazed at how many people do not clean the drain or the drain basket. Those areas should get special attention. Scrub the drain and drain basket with a brush and a good disinfectant cleaner. Throw the basket in the dishwasher once in awhile to keep it germ-free.

Sink Kickin Boogie

If you don't have a dishwasher, give your legs a workout while your hands are busy at the kitchen sink. Alternate between side and back kicks.

Counters

If countertops were clutter-free, cleaning them would be easy.

How to clean countertops varies with the type of surface. They can be made of wood, ceramic tile, Corian®, stainless steel, granite and other materials.

All countertops should have everything removed from them once a week. Clean them with a good disinfectant. Remember to dry them.

If the countertop has a rough surface, use a soft brush to clean the "pits." The same method is used if you have ceramic tile. Use a soft brush to clean the grout. When this hasn't been done, the accumulated dirt can actually change the countertop color.

To remove stains from countertops—
- use a bleach solution, rinse and dry for Formica®.
- use a cleanser and a scrubby on Corian®.
- check manufacturer's directions for all other surfaces.

I recommend no harsh abrasives. They can leave your countertop scratched and more prone to future stains. Wipe up spills immediately so they don't harden, clean and buff to a nice shine. Your countertops will look beautiful for a long time.

Clara's CLEANING SCRUB

Mix together 1-3/4 to 2 cups baking soda with 1/2 cup (or 4 oz) of a liquid castile soap which you'll find in a health food—not a grocery—store. Add 1/2 cup water and 3 Tbsp vinegar. Stir in a container until the mixture is smooth. Add a drop of scented oil or flavoring for fragrance. *(I like to use Dr. Bronner's Peppermint Pure-Castile Soap as it eliminates the need to add anything else.)* Pour and store in a clean ketchup bottle with a squirt top and cap, or something similar. Shake well before using. It's the perfect mild-abrasive, neutral cleaner that is great on ceramics, painted cabinets, stainless steel, stove tops, tubs, tile, and even glass coffee carafes.

Refrigerators

Most newer model refrigerators have a rough finish on the doors to help hide fingerprints. But, the prints are still there. Make sure to wipe behind the handles, and open the doors to clean the door edges. While the door is open, wipe off lower shelves and any obvious spills. You may need a step stool to clean the top of the refrigerator, but the extra effort is worth it—especially if you have any guests six feet or taller. Clean once a week.

About once a month, the lower grate of the refrigerator should be removed and washed. The cooling "fins," or what looks like a series of parallel metal plates, collect dust. They must be vacuumed for the refrigerator to work most efficiently.

Periodically—every couple of months—the complete interior of the refrigerator should be cleaned. At that time, take out and wash all shelves, trays, etc. Don't forget to clean the rubber seal around the refrigerator door.

In a frost-free refrigerator, there's (generally) a shallow pan underneath the unit, on the freezer side. The pan catches condensation. It's easy to wash it out with warm water and detergent. The hard part is remembering to do the job. To help you remember, mark your calendar with "Ref. Pan," once a month. With that cleaning schedule, you won't have to worry about refrigerator odors.

A good cleaning solution for the inside of the refrigerator consists of three tablespoons of baking soda, dissolved in a quart of warm water. It'll do a good job of cleaning and deodorizing the refrigerator. After cleaning, leave a box of baking soda (with the top removed, or the vented box) in the refrigerator to absorb odors. Another idea for a nice, clean smell is to pour a little vanilla or wintergreen extract on a piece of cotton. Place the cotton in a glass dish on the bottom refrigerator shelf.

Stoves

There are three basic types of range tops available on stoves. They are gas, electric and ceramic.

Gas & Electric Ranges

Weekly cleaning for gas and electric ranges should consist of washing and drying the entire exterior. Remove the knobs to make the job easier.

Wash reflector bowls/drip pans by soaking them in warm soapsuds. Wipe spills from the surface underneath the heating units. Many stovetops can be raised for access to the area under the burners. Some people like to line their reflector bowls with foil to save time in cleaning.

Do not submerge electrical burners in water. They are self-cleaning.

Ceramic Stovetops

This top is a variation of the electric range, with elements hidden underneath marked surfaces. While the smooth range top appears easy to clean, it needs special care. It's easy to damage or discolor the ceramic surface. Be sure to read the cleaning instructions that came with the unit. If you don't have them, try the following:

• Always make sure the surface is cool before you clean it.

• Sprinkle the surface with a non-abrasive cleanser or *Clara's* Cleaning Scrub and rub gently with a sponge. Rinse well with clear water, and dry with a soft cloth.

Rag Doll Rag

Take a deep breath and reach for the ceiling. Raise your arms over your head. Keep reaching for the ceiling. Do this five times to warm up, or after doing any chore that keeps you bent over. It gets your circulation moving and is wonderful for tension relief.

Microwave

I don't turn on other's appliances so I use a spray-on degreaser and let it sit awhile before wiping clean. You may prefer to just steam up the insides by boiling some water and baking soda in a glass container. Then interior wipes clean without any need to scrub.

Oven

Unless you are fortunate enough to have a self-cleaning oven, or a housecleaning service, there comes a day when your oven must be cleaned.

For a quick cleanup of caked-on spills—but not for self-cleaning or continuous-cleaning ovens—use a damp pumice stone.

Many strong, commercial cleaning products are designed to work in standard ovens. Most oven cleaners are dangerous if they touch your skin or eyes. Wear rubber gloves to protect your hands, and follow all product safety precautions.

Apply oven cleaner to your electric oven the night before cleaning. Avoid getting the oven-cleaner spray on surrounding surfaces. Protect the floor with newspaper in case any oven cleaner leaks out during the night. Cover the heating elements with foil if they are not removable. Remove racks, broiler pan and drip pans (if they are removable and cannot be harmed by oven cleaner). Spray all with oven cleaner, place inside a garbage bag and tie shut. Leave them overnight before rinsing clean.

Make sure to remove the oven cleaner residue. Put vinegar in the last rinse water so your oven doesn't smell like burnt cleaner next time it's turned up.

Don't use any abrasive cleaner on the glass in the oven door.

If a casserole, pie, etc. bubbles over in the oven, quickly sprinkle the spill with salt. When the oven is cool, wipe out burnt food with a damp sponge.

For self-cleaning ovens, follow manufacturer's directions.

Range Hoods

Most stoves have separate, or built-in, range hoods above their work surfaces. Range hoods are usually vented to the outside. They remove grease, steam and cooking odors from the kitchen. However, some hoods do not have outside vents. They rely on special, replaceable filters to remove smoke and odors. Both kinds of hoods need regular cleaning to keep them grease-free and effective.

Wipe off the exterior and interior of range hoods every week. Remove the filter and wash in a degreaser solution or run through the dishwasher. Allow drying time before replacing the filter. Wipe the blades of the fan without removing them. Clean the metal, mesh filters monthly. Replace special filters on non-vented hoods every six months.

Do not use an abrasive cleanser on any part of the hood. What you need for the job is a degreaser, which as the name implies, removes the grease. Formula 409® or Fantastic® are all-purpose cleaners that work well as degreasers.

Wipe spills promptly. Then, make it a habit to clean the stove top every time you do the dishes.

Dishwasher

The dishwasher isn't as hard to keep up as a stove or refrigerator. If you have a dishwasher, or plan on getting one, consider installing a water softener. (If you live in a hard water area of the country, it's a worthwhile investment.)

Have you ever been in a home where the dishwasher interior was all brown? The stains are caused by iron and lime deposits, the result of hard water. If you don't have a water softener and your dishwasher has already turned brown, there is still hope! Some grocery stores carry dishwasher cleaner.

To do the most thorough cleaning job on your dishwasher, apply phosphoric acid cleaner (see page 86) with your bowl swab (or "johnny mop," described on page 53). Let it sit for ten minutes, then run the rinse cycle.

I haven't tried it, but another popular suggestion for removing lime buildup is to run Tang™—or an equivalent—through a rinse cycle. The citric acid helps eliminate discoloration.

Electric Can Opener

Yes, your electric can opener needs regular, but fortunately minimal, care.

- Always unplug before cleaning.

- Never immerse the case in water.

- Wipe off after each use to remove food residue.

- Once in awhile, remove the cutting wheel and lid-cover, and soak them in hot, sudsy water.

- Scrub caked-on food with an old toothbrush.

- Run a wet paper towel through it for one turn of the cutting wheel. (Even a handheld can opener can be cleaned this way.)

Toaster

All toasters need regular attention to keep them clean, shiny and crumb-free. If you use it daily, clean it weekly.

- Always unplug before cleaning.

- Never immerse the toaster in water.

- Use baking soda to clean the exterior, since it won't scratch metal surfaces.

- Remove the crumb tray at the base of the toaster and shake out accumulated crumbs. Wash the tray in warm soapsuds.

- If it has no crumb tray, turn the toaster upside down. Shake the crumbs into the sink. Then use a thin soft brush to remove crumbs from the interior. Sometimes an old toothbrush does the trick.

Floors

Floors come in a variety materials. Knowing the specific materials of the floor is an important factor in their care. Using the wrong cleaning method or product can damage some floors. The following directions apply to all floors, except carpeting.

- Wipe up spills and sticky spots immediately.

- Be careful moving furniture across floors.

- Protect heavy-traffic areas with mats or throw rugs.

- Sweep, dust mop, or vacuum heavy-traffic areas regularly.

Unless you are using a product (such as Damp Mop—page 87) that tells you not to dry your floor, you should dry the floor. Otherwise, most cleaners leave a residue that that will dull the look of your floor over time.

Dirty Dancing

Wipe dry your kitchen floor with a small towel under each foot. Put on your favorite music and make it a fun excercise.

Chapter 4

Will This (Living) Room Come to Order?

On one of my first cleaning jobs, a man asked me to please hand-wash his woolen underwear. I promptly washed them, stretched and shaped them, then laid them out to dry on his dining room table. It was just like I'd been taught to wash and dry my sweaters on our family's Formica® table.

The man called me that evening and thanked me for washing the underwear and asked me if I realized where I had put them. "Yessir!" I replied. "They're right there on your dining room table." He politely educated me on the interaction of water and wood.

The following day, on his dining room table, next to the outline of his underwear, was some rubbing compound. Also there were written instructions to apply the compound and rub for fifteen minutes each time I came to clean. It took about a month, but I finally restored the table so he could eat without looking at his underwear outlines.

Living Room/Family Room

Whatever you call it, one of the most-used rooms of your house needs thorough attention once a week. The step-by-step instructions given make the job easier. Don't get overwhelmed. It's easy once you know the basics.

Storage

To those who ask, "Where can I store things in my living room?" I suggest footstools with lift-up lids and end tables with drawers. Yes, Queen Anne tables or parson's tables are lovely, but there's no place to keep stuff.

- If you have bookcases, try adding doors to the bottom shelves. Those shelves are inconvenient for books and are a target for dust. Don't install louvered doors on the bookcases, or anywhere else in your home, for that matter. You're much too busy to clean louvers.

- Under the sofa, if there's room, use a large, flat plastic storage container (otherwise known as an under-bed box). Use it for storing hide-a-bed linens or other seldom-used items.

- Display favorite knickknacks in a glass-topped curio table or cabinet. It permits you to enjoy them without weekly dusting.

- Use arm and headrest area covers to protect your upholstered furniture from body and hair oils. Look for nice quality cloth napkins to match or coordinate with existing fabrics.

Windows & Screens

The secret to the cleanest windows is in the drying, not the washing. Always dry windows with 100% cotton. Buy old sheets and cotton T-shirts at garage sales if you need extra rags.

If you have family members who smoke, or little ones who like to look out the windows, wash your windows at least once a month. Do fingerprint touch-up as necessary.

When this chore finally does come due, keep these important tips in mind:

- Always use window cleaner, never soap. You can make your own window cleaner using a capful of Murphy® Oil Soap (which isn't really soap!) and two quarts of water.

- Make a window washing solution with a half-cup ammonia and two tablespoons vinegar mixed in a bucket of warm water.

- Never wash windows when the sun is shining directly on them. The windows dry too fast and show streaks.

- When drying windows, use vertical strokes on the inside and horizontal strokes on the outside, or vice-versa. This simple method helps you find which side has the "wipe-lines," if either.

- When Jack Frost comes, wash your windows by adding a half-cup of rubbing alcohol or windshield washer solution to every quart of wash water.

- As weather permits, open the windows. Remember to clean the windowsills and the inside ledge between screen and glass. Also clean the tracks of sliding glass doors.

Side Swipe Wipe

For waistline perfection, and a clearer reflection, try this window washing stretch. Begin with knees slightly bent, left hand on waist and a cleaning cloth (or sponge) in your right hand. Stretch to the left and back again. Do this 20 to 30 times, then switch sides.

Clean windowsills according to the surface finish. Painted sills are cleaned with a neutral cleaner. Varnished surfaces are cleaned with Murphy® Oil Soap, then oiled.

- The window's inside ledge should be cleaned summer, spring and fall. It helps keep pollen and dust from blowing inside open windows. Leave that area alone during the winter.

- Window screens are collectors of dust and dirt. If the dirt isn't removed, it's transferred to your windows when it rains. Screens that are on the inside don't collect as much dust as outside ones, but they still should be kept clean.

One way of cleaning screens is to use kerosene. (It's easy to buy small bottles packaged as candlewick fluid.) Dampen a rag in kerosene and rub both sides of the mesh and the frames.

Any all-purpose cleaner works nearly as well as kerosene. Apply the cleaner with a brush to both sides of the screen. Rinse well with clear water. It's best to do this cleaning outside, on a cement surface. Use your garden hose to rinse the screens off.

> Use the same technique—a rag dampened with kerosene—to give your car an occasional waterless wash.

Floors

Since most family rooms are carpeted or have wood floors, they're the two surfaces with cleaning directions here.

Before Vacuuming:
- Pick up any sharp or hard items, like paper clips or pins. They can damage belt, bag or hose.

> Pick up small objects such as pins, buttons or screws. Drop them into a plastic bag you keep attached to the vacuum for that purpose. Occasionally sort and put away objects.

- Check the dust bag and replace, or empty it, if almost full.

You'll get better cleaning efficiency and motor protection, since motors cool by circulating air.

- Make sure the dust bag is properly in place. An improper fitting would defeat the purpose entirely.

- Remove threads or hair from the rotating agitator brushes. It improves efficiency of the brushes.

- Adjust the nozzle height of an upright to the rug pile if the cleaner doesn't adjust automatically. The nozzle should ridge just above the carpet pile. Too low an adjustment makes the cleaner hard to push and causes accelerated wear on the rug. Too high an adjustment won't give the rug a deep cleaning.

- Check the belt that runs the agitator. When it is stretched or starting to wear thin, it won't work properly. Replace the belt, following directions from the owner's manual, or have it done at a repair shop.

Occasionally:
- Clean the tools, filters and housing, following directions from your owner's manual.

- Check brushes for wear. They should extend just below the edges of the nozzle. Adjust down, if adjustable.

> For a longer cleaning range, add a twelve-foot extension cord. It'll let you clean up to an extra thirty-foot radius before you need another outlet.

When finished vacuuming:
- Store the vacuum in a dry place.

- Keep the hose on a shelf, or hang it over two hooks, spaced well apart to keep the hose from crimping.

Cleaning Difficult Carpet Styles

Deep pile rugs are difficult to clean at the bottom where destructive, embedded dirt hides. Sculptured rugs pose the same problems as those of deep pile, only more so, with the peak-valley cut of the pile. Shag rugs create a similar problem. An additional problem occurs when strings get tangled in the beater bar. The solution is to set the vacuum cleaner lower than feels comfortable. You needn't do this extra pushing action every time you vacuum.

Don't shake oriental or braided rugs. Shaking causes the "structural" threads to break. Instead, carefully vacuum with a canister vac.

Blot—never wipe up—spills on carpets. For remaining wetness, place some clean rags or towels over the area and top with a few heavy books. Leave for awhile to "wick" up moisture.

Wood Floors

Wood floors are beautiful when properly cared for. Expect extra work to get and keep them in that condition.

There are two types of wood floors—sealed and unsealed. A

sealed floor is coated with varnish, urethane or other sealer. It always looks shiny and should never need to be polished. To clean, apply a neutral cleaner or a Murphy® Oil Soap solution with a well-wrung-out rag. Wipe dry.

An unsealed floor has no protective coating on it. It has an oil or stain finish. Don't use water on this type of floor! Use a cleaner made especially for hardwood floors, such as Bruce's® Hardwood Floor Cleaner. When applying the cleaner, always work with the grain of the wood. Some waxes require a buffer. Avoid that step by using a one-step wax. Be sure to read the directions on the packaging. Wax two or three times a year.

Fireplaces

When a fireplace needs cleaning, make it the first job in that room. Do it first because it raises dust and dirt that settle on furniture and tables.

Use newspaper to protect the hearth and carpeting. Many fireplaces have small holes in the back and bottom, to sweep the ashes into. If not, remove the ashes with a small shovel. Put the (cold) ashes in a bag. Keep the dust down by sprinkling or misting the ashes with water. (Leave a small bed of ashes for easier fire starting and easier burning.)

At season's end, if you want to vacuum the fireplace, put a damp cloth over the vacuum's vent. Otherwise, ash and dust could escape the vacuum's filter. The damp cloth catches soot before it settles on the furniture.

Clean fireplace glass doors with an ammonia-vinegar solution or a good degreaser solution. Never use an abrasive cleaner or scouring pad on the glass!

Before cleaning the smoke or soot stains from the fireplace front, determine if it's unsealed brick or a soft flagstone. If you're not careful, wet cleaners drive the dirt in deeper on porous (unsealed) surfaces. If the surface is hard and non-porous, clean it with a vinegar solution.

On non-porous brick, use a brush and scrub well. Wipe as quickly as possible. A solution of one cup of trisodium phosphate to one gallon of water works well, too.

For soft or porous brick, vacuum thoroughly. For stubborn spots, rub with an art-gum eraser.

Cut down on soot, and needing to scrub the fireplace front, by occasionally throwing a little salt on the burning logs.

> For a pleasant, spicy aroma, put a few dried lemon or orange rinds in with the logs when you build your next fire.

Don't burn the comics or ad sections! Use crumpled black and white newspapers only. Colored inks, when burned, release measurable amounts of lead into the air. Everything doesn't go up the chimney, and it's not what you want to breathe.

Heat Vents

If you have forced-air heat, clean the louvered vents occasionally. Vacuum them with a floor brush, or damp sponge them. For a thorough job, take the vents off the wall and wash them in the sink. Once they're clean, you'll get more heat and less dust blowing around.

Cut down on duct dust by stretching a piece of cheesecloth behind the vents.

Pianos

A piano is an expensive piece of furniture and should be treated with care! Keep the lid of a grand piano closed when the piano isn't in use.

Remove stains from the piano keys with a paste of baking soda and water. Dip a damp cloth in the paste, and rub gently until clean. Don't let the mixture fall between the keys! Don't place your piano in direct sunlight. Don't cover the keyboard if the keys are made of ivory—they could turn yellow. Wipe the case with a cloth dampened in a Murphy® Oil Soap solution. Wipe dry. If the piano has a real wood finish, treat it to an application of oil occasionally.

Books

Dust books at least once a month with the vacuum brush attachment. Yearly, remove all books from the shelves and wipe them with a (barely) damp cloth. And, don't crowd your books. Like clothes hanging in the closet, they need room to breathe. Try to keep your books away from direct sunlight. The sun can make covers fade and deteriorate. If any of your books have leather covers, treat them to a light application of oil once a year.

Television Sets

As much as we watch television, we should notice when it needs cleaning, but most people don't. It is, along with the telephone, one of the most-often-missed items when a house is cleaned.

Clean the TV screen with window cleaner, but spray it on the cloth, not the screen! Cleaner causes damage if it seeps behind the glass. Use a soft toothbrush to clean the small crevices. Your TV should be cleaned weekly.

In short, the weekly chores for cleaning a much-used family or living room are:

- Dust furniture and everything on the furniture.
- Check under cushions, and vacuum if necessary.
- Wipe windows of fingerprints.
- Spot clean walls, especially around light switches.
- Move small furniture, and vacuum carpet.
- Wipe mirrors and pictures.

Chapter 5

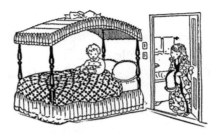

Bath, Bed and Beyond

Domestic Engineering clients often lose things and ask us to keep an eye out for them while we are cleaning. We have found diamonds, cash and lots of other things with sentimental or monetary value.

"Keep an eye out for my boa constrictor," is a request we only got once. The homeowner explained to us in a very calm manner that the snake had somehow gotten out of its cage and was "somewhere loose in the house."

Armed with broomsticks and vacuum attachments, our cleaners worked side by side. No crafty snake was going to separate them and devour them individually. Together they snuck up on windowsills and furniture cushions.

The workers tried to think like a reptile. Would a hungry snake coil in a chandelier ready to pounce on a tasty cleaning person? Or hide by a door waiting for a chance to slither to freedom? After all, he'd already broken out of his cage.

While emptying the garbage can from under the sink, they found the missing snake. Not much keeps our cleaning people from completing a task, but being eye-to-eye with a boa constrictor kept that garbage right where it was.

Bathrooms

Most bathrooms were not designed for all the equipment we use today. Shavers, hairdryers, hair curlers and hygiene products all add to a huge bathroom inventory.

- A shelf under the sink goes a long way toward reducing the clutter and making your bathroom look neater.

- Extra toilet tissue and shampoo should be stored in the bathroom. If possible, store washcloths and towels in the bathroom. (I know one person who stores linen in her dining room hutch! Fortunately, it's a small home so it's near the bathroom.)

- Remove the wrappers from a couple bars of soap and put them on your bathroom shelves. The smell freshens the room, and the dried soap lasts longer.

- Store small waste-can liners or bags in the bottom of the trashcan in the bathroom. They'll be out of sight, but handy, under the liner that's in use.

- A wall clock in the bathroom helps keep dawdlers on schedule, especially during the morning "rush hour." Battery-operated clocks are sold in sizes and styles to suit any bathroom.

Don't buy paper towels that claim they can absorb the Mississippi River. They leave lint all over everything. For cleaning, buy the cheapest brand you can find. For the environment, buy the towels that tear off in half-size sheets.

- Install a paper-towel holder in the bathroom to keep your bathroom cleaner. You'll find many uses for them. They're especially helpful with daily spiffing up chores, such as cleaning the mirror and wiping the chrome.

- To prevent staining on medicine cabinet shelves, wax the shelves.

Toilet

Toilet cleaning is easier when the water is out of the bowl. To get the water out, dump a pailful of water into the toilet. It'll actually empty and not refill, leaving it ready to clean. (This won't work on "tankless" toilets.)

- Use a commercial cleaner for cleaning the toilet bowl. (There are tank products that do very little cleaning while turning the water blue. The problem is, the blue water sometimes stains the bowl.)

- Remove blue water and other waterline stains with a pumice stone made for that purpose. A pumice stone is to be used wet. Leave the water in the bowl while you rub at the stains until they are "erased." Pumice stone is a mild abrasive that isn't harmful to porcelain. You won't need to use it every week.

- Clean the exterior of the toilet with the same product you use on your sink and tub. Protect your hands with rubber gloves.

As a professional cleaner, I don't use the toilet brushes you find in most stores. I use bowl swabs. Swabs are not brushes or sponges, but something in between. They have handles like a toilet brush. Instead of stiff brush material, they have a soft, synthetic, cloth-like head. (Bowl swabs are sometimes called "johnny mops.")

Bowl swabs aren't readily available from retailers, though some large hardware stores carry them. They're available from janitorial supply houses or by mail order (see page 113).

By thrusting a swab down the "throat," or drainage hole, of a toilet you can actually remove all the water from the bowl. With the swab, "push" the water down the toilet's throat. It might take six to twelve strokes to empty the bowl, but the water will leave.

Now, your toilet bowl cleaner works more effectively because it isn't diluted.

Using swabs also means no unsightly brush and holder gathering dust and gunk in the bathroom. The bowl swab can be rinsed and hung on a hook out of sight. You can also buy toilet swabs that have a built-in wringer/cover.

Johnny mop (swabs) can be used to clean hard-to-get-at places not found in the bathroom, such as between appliances and counters, on louvered doors and on mini-blinds.

Shower Curtains and Doors

If you use a shower curtain, buy a cheap liner. Treat it like it's disposable. Throw the liner away when it gets mildewed. Use a spray mildew inhibitor on the inside of a more expensive shower curtain. (Yes, shower curtains and/or liners can be laundered and dried on low heat with a few towels, but why bother?)

Wall Flower Waltz

When cleaning the walls, in a kneeling position, stretch toward the ceiling, trying to get one hand higher than the other, as though you are reaching for the stars. Do five reaches initially and work up to ten. Stand and repeat. By then the walls should be sparkling!

Glass shower doors represent a cleaning challenge if you allow hard water deposits to build up.

- As needed, use a commercial metal and tile cleaner. Apply with a bowl swab (johnny mop), rinse and wipe clean.

- After thoroughly cleaning the shower door, apply a light coat of lemon oil.

The trick is to prevent deposits from building up on the glass. The mineral deposits in the water time will eventually etch the glass. To avoid that, get in the squeegee habit. Squeegees are widely available. If there isn't one in your bathroom, there should be.

Squeegee the shower doors after each use, and train your family to do the same. After showering, run the blade down the walls quickly. Tiles dry spot-free.

If you squeegee doors (or tiles) before you get out of the shower, but (obviously) after you turn the water off, you can air-dry a bit, saving on floor cleanup. Your less-wet towel dries faster, too.

Leave shower doors partly open when not in use. Air circulation retards mildew growth.

You can also use your shower squeegee to clean countertops, mirrors and tiles. It can even be used to gather up table crumbs.

Bathtubs

Everyone likes to take a bath, but no one likes to clean the tub!

Most bathtubs are made of enameled steel or cast iron and can be cleaned with any heavy-duty bathroom cleaner. Products such as Soft Scrub® can also be used, just don't scrub too hard or use an abrasive cleaning pad. If you feel you must use a scrubbing pad, please rub gently.

I prefer a phosphoric acid cleaner. It's a liquid which I apply with a bowl swab, let set for five minutes, rinse, dry, and the job's done. Phosphoric acid cleaner is a cleaner that you would not want to use as a daily cleaner, but as a now-and-then cleaner it can't be beat.

Using bath oil in your bath water helps to keep the soap scum from adhering to the tub. After your bath, wipe the tub dry with your bath towel.

If your tub is made of fiberglass, a little more care must be taken. The shiny surface of fiberglass is quite soil-resistant if you can keep it intact. This means you can't use abrasive cleaners of any kind. If a good neutral cleaner and a soft cleaning pad don't do the job, try a liquid cleanser. Rub carefully.

Use bleach to remove the mildew on tub and shower enclosures. (But remember, if it's sealed grout, bleach can cause the sealer to deteriorate. Rinse well.) There are many good cleaning products that contain bleach. Or you can make your own of one part bleach to five parts water. Apply the solution, and scrub with a good, stiff grout brush. Rinse well, and dry.

Tile

When you mention the word tile, most people think of ceramic tile. However, there are many different kinds of tile. Tile can be made of vinyl, clay, asphalt, or stone, just to mention a few. But, the average homeowner has ceramic tile. That's the tile I'll address.

Ceramic tile is usually glazed, with a beautiful finish. It'll resist staining and soiling. People install it in showers, walls, floors and countertops. The only problem with tile is that it must be grouted. Grouting can be difficult to keep clean. (See next page.)

Most of the time, all you need to do to ceramic floors is to damp clean with a neutral cleaner. If the ceramic has a high-gloss finish, dry the floor. It will prevent any buildup, and the floor maintains its beautiful shine.

Soap scum and hard water deposits come off easily with a

phosphoric acid cleaner. Apply with a bowl swab, let set, rinse well, and squeegee dry. If you find that you must use a cleaning pad, make sure it's not too abrasive. Scrub lightly so you don't harm the glossy surface.

Grout

Grout gets stained, dirty, and worst of all, mildewed. It's what makes cleaning ceramic tile walls, floors and countertops so difficult. If we could eliminate grout, we could really cut cleaning time.

When having new grout installed, make sure it's sealed well. Years ago people didn't seal grout, which is why there's lots of mildew in older homes. There are good sealers available. Before using any sealer, it's important to clean the old grout with a ceramic cleaner. Your local tile store will be happy to help you with those two items.

Weekly Bathroom Chores

- Wipe the windows and walls, clean the floor and empty the trashcan.
- Wash and polish dry mirrors.
- Clean sink and polish chrome.
- Clean tile and tub. Don't use a powdered cleanser to clean the tub, as its residue can irritate delicate areas of bathers.
- Clean toilet stool, inside and out.

Bedrooms

The key to bedroom organization is using storage space wisely.

- Don't let the space beneath your bed go to waste. Flat garment boxes with lids can be used to store winter clothes, extra blankets, etc.

- Both bed and sofa pillows perk up and smell nice after a trip through the dryer. Add a fabric softener sheet.

Sheet Beat Stretch

Bend and stretch from the waist when making beds or picking up objects from the floor. Don't lock your knees, though. Keep knees slightly bent.

- Handle heating pads and electric blankets with care. Don't fold or crease them or tuck them under the mattress edge. Don't have electric blankets dry-cleaned.

Keep beverage coasters in the bedroom to prevent furniture spotting and staining of wooden night tables and dressers.

- Wash curtains with a few drops of perfume in the final rinse water. Between drycleanings, draperies can go into the dryer with a damp bath towel. Leave plenty of room for fluffing—don't crowd curtains in the dryer. Re-hang drapes immediately so wrinkles hang out.

- Use shoe racks for storing your shoes on the floor. They can be moved for cleaning closet floors. Some door shoe racks can also be attached to closet walls.

- If you can find the room, store the sheets and pillowcases in the bedroom where they are to be used. It's not only sensible, but saves many steps! You could also store an extra blanket between the box spring and mattress of each bed. They're out of the way until needed again.

- Keep several wicker baskets or pretty boxes to collect those things that your family tends to leave laying around.

- Wipe bare floors with a damp cloth or mop.

Weekly Bedroom Chores

Apply the weekly living room instructions, and add:
- Change bed linens.
- Shake throw rugs.
- Empty garbage cans.

That covers cleaning more than half of most homes. Now let's cover the rest of the house.

Chapter 6

I Kid You Not! Children's Rooms

We never know what to expect when cleaning a child's room, so we appreciate it when a parent warns us of anything out of the ordinary.

One mother left us a note saying that, in her son's bedroom, we should "work around the car parts." Hubcaps, headlights, that sort of thing, came to mind.

We found those, along with fenders, exhaust pipes, bumpers, tires and a battery—among other things. In fact, her son was well on his way to assembling an entire Chevy in his bedroom! Nothing personal, but we don't want to clean that house the day after Junior drives his car out the front door.

Children's Rooms

If you want children to clean their rooms, you must teach them how. It's easy to tell a child, "Go clean your room." But it's on a par with someone telling you to "Fly this plane" if you've had no training. Don't let your child flounder with a vague order or veiled threats. When you're a parent, you're also a teacher.

Teaching our young people to clean enables them to live in harmony with themselves and their surroundings. The ability to take responsibility for themselves and their quarters is one of the most useful tools for living we can give a child—one which makes a real difference in children becoming happier, more productive and creative adults.

We teach sex education, cooking and sewing, but nothing about cleaning. Yet, nothing contributes more to good physical and mental health than clean surroundings. A recent study by the University of Michigan School of Social Work, as reported in *Good Housekeeping*, found that "kids raised in clean homes— regardless of their intellectual ability or parents' household in- come—stick with school longer and earn more money as adults than those raised with dust bunnies."

As their cleanliness/neatness teacher, decide on the level of cleanliness you want in your child's room. It should be roughly the same standard as the rest of the house. Not much better, not much worse.

Your attitude is mirrored back to you by your child. So avoid complaining about how hard it is to keep everything clean, or your child won't want to do the work any more than you do.

Then go into the child's room. Sit in the middle of the room on the floor or on a small chair. Now that you have your child's perspective of the room, ask yourself these questions:

- Is this room easy to pick up and clean?
- Is the bed easy to make?
- Is the room filled with too much stuff or toys?
- Are there too many clothes out and about?
- Does this room have adequate storage?
- Can the tasks be broken into child-manageable jobs?

Patterned carpet in kids' rooms helps hide spills and stains. Carpet also makes the room more sound-proof than other flooring options.

Beds

Is the bed filled with stuffed toys? Are there too many blankets and pillows? Is the bed far enough away from the wall so the child can move around it easily?

Avoid bunk beds if you can. They are very difficult for a child to make.

Bunk beds or not, washable comforters or duvets instead of blankets and bedspreads help. Also, assign each household member a certain color of linens. That way sheets and towels can readily be sent to the right room, and children can identify their own linens. Color coding works for organizing kids!

Discourage relatives from giving more stuffed animals to your child. These animals seem to multiply in the night. Store excess stuffed toys in a mesh bag hung from the ceiling or from wall hooks. There's a hanging plastic chain with clasps specifically designed for holding toys, hats and so on.

Litterbug Jitterbug

Picking up toys can be a time to tone up your body. To tone your waist, always bend from the middle and stretch to reach objects in low places. Keep your knees slightly bent.

Toys

Don't purchase more or bigger toy boxes. A child always wants the toy on the bottom of the box, so the toys on top land on the floor. Boxes on shelves are better and safer as a storage option for kids' toys.

Dispose of the toys that are broken or have missing pieces. Toss also any toy your child no longer plays with. Box the "disposal" toys and store them for a while, out of sight. If your child doesn't miss them, throw the box out.

Purging the toy box is a parent's, not child's, job. A child only parts with his sibling's toys.

Buy open, colored bins to store the remaining toys. Label each container with the name of the item it's supposed to store. For youngsters who don't yet read, attach a picture of the item to the container. Now you can teach children to put things away, because there's a designated place to put things.

Clothes

Again dispose of outdated, outgrown, or unused items. Typically, the leftovers are a few outfits that the child wears often. Don't fight it! The fewer clothes children have to pick from, the easier it is for them to coordinate an outfit and dress without assistance.

Use hangers and place out-of-season pieces in the back of the closet. For the daily wear, install hooks and pegs on closet walls. Get each child a hamper or basket for dirty clothes. A child old enough to toddle can learn to put clothes in a hamper.

Storage

Make sure there are plenty of low shelves, drawers and cabinets for the children to store their books, clothes and "good junk." Check the drawers and doors of storage areas to make certain that they open and close readily. Anything that's difficult to get into probably won't be used. Small plastic bins that fit on shelves work well.

If your child is a collector of small trinkets, dolls, etc., get a glass-doored cabinet for display and dust control. Another good investment is a bulletin board. Kids like to see their awards, school papers and posters hung up. Think about covering one whole wall with corkboard. You can even buy "chalkboard" paint for one wall, or turn one or more walls into ongoing works of art.

Furniture in children's rooms should be washable. Walls, too, need durable, washable paint or washable wallpaper.

Give children the responsibility of keeping their rooms clean and organized. It's a relatively simple chore once you make the room child-friendly. And remember, shutting the door to your child's room and ignoring the mess is, in my opinion, an exercise in futility. It does nothing to teach your child about living an orderly life.

Chapter 7

And Now, the Rest of the Story

A young man called to ask if he could possibly get his apartment cleaned the next day. Workers were available, so a preview was attempted. He was leaving town, but trusted us and would leave a check. If everything worked out, he said, he'd like to be put on a regular cleaning schedule. Reluctantly, the cleaning was scheduled, sight unseen.

Our cleaning people looked for cleaning supplies, then the check (which they would pick up when the job was complete). They found neither supplies nor the check!

Then one of the women heard footsteps in the supposedly vacant apartment. She turned to see a naked man who demanded to know what she was doing there. Keeping her eyes glued to his face, she gracefully exited the apartment backwards, babbling all the way.

We no longer make exceptions to the home interview policy. And we don't accept "clothing optional" jobs.

Dining Room

The dining room, closets, halls and laundry room aren't necessarily weekly tasks except as a "once over." It depends on how you use those areas.

The following rules of thumb apply to dining rooms used as formal rooms, and not to those used daily or those used as craft rooms.

- Dining room furniture should be washable. Then, wash it twice a year.
- Cover chair cushions in a material that hides spots and stains. Prints or patterns work best.
- Keep a rug under the table whether the room is carpeted or has wood flooring. A stained area rug is much less costly to replace than a carpet.
- Twice a year remove, clean and replace everything in the china hutch.

Heat marks on furniture caused by hot coffee cups or dishes can usually be removed with a cloth dampened with peppermint oil, camphor oil or linseed oil. Rub lightly with the grain of the wood.

Water spots caused by glasses or flower vases can usually be removed using a mild abrasive mixture. Mix white toothpaste or another lubricant with water. Make a paste, then gently rub the stained finish along the grain of the wood. Rub until the spot blends with the surrounding area. Re-wax and oil immediately.

- Keep several sets of coasters around to be used whenever liquids are served. Watermarks are notoriously difficult to remove.

- One way to avoid damaging beautiful wood tabletops is to cover the surface with a tablecloth, then top with a custom cut piece of glass. (It won't hurt the wood, just be careful not to get liquids—including cleaning products—between the glass and the table.)

Chandeliers

Chandeliers fall into the periodic cleaning category. Start by either moving your dining room table or covering it with a blanket or old towel. It prevents your table from being scratched, should you accidentally drop anything. Some folks also hook an open, inverted umbrella from the chandelier to protect the table or floor.

Use an ammonia-water-vinegar solution to clean it. (It's the same solution for cleaning windows.) Wipe and dry each piece of the chandelier. Don't keep turning the chandelier in one direction as you clean. Chandeliers are usually screwed into the ceiling, so turning in one direction could loosen the screw and cause the chandelier to fall. To be safe, clean half of the chandelier, then reverse the direction. Spray-on chandelier cleaners are more expensive and less effective than the ammonia/water/vinegar solution.

Make sure the light bulbs are cool, and light is turned off, before attempting to clean a chandelier.

Getting some of those harder-to-clean surfaces in good condition makes them easier to maintain.

Halls & Entries

The hall in the most-used entry is a good place to keep boxes labeled for each family member. As you clean and pick up the house, you can put all the items that are out of place into the boxes. When anyone says, "Where did you put my stuff," you can say, "If it isn't in your box, I don't know."

- Boot trays are an excellent way to keep mud off the hall floor.

- Put a grass-type mat outside your door and a rug or mat just inside the entry. It'll keep a large percentage of the outside dirt from coming inside.

Slate

Slate flooring is used frequently in entry areas. This means it's subject to a great deal of gritty dirt. Slate should be washed frequently with a neutral cleaner to prevent scratching from small abrasive particles. If you like a shiny finish, you can apply a dressing about every three months. The dressing can be purchased at most flooring stores. Be careful not to over-wax slate. It can cause a chalky buildup.

Closets

There are two issues with a closet. One is keeping it organized, and the other is keeping it cleaned. If you do both on a regular basis you won't feel you have to move every couple of years.

Bedroom Closets

Organization is the word to keep in mind for your clothes closet. Start with a few large, plastic garbage or leaf bags. Set aside one of them for items to be repaired.

- Take everything out of the closet and hope no one comes to the front door. Throw away whatever you don't think you'll ever need or use, or haven't worn for twelve to eighteen months. If items are in good shape, set them aside, pack them up and drive to the nearest donation center. It's for your own good, and it's a tax write-off.

- Wipe down walls and wash or vacuum the floor before returning anything to the closet.

Children's closets should have low rods and an assortment of substantial hooks at their eye level so that the little ones can reach them. It'll encourage them to hang their clothes by themselves.

- Also, before you replace anything in the closet, remember that stores have many sizes of storage boxes for shoes, sweaters and other items. They also have garment bags, various types of wall hooks and space-saver bins for the shelves and floor. Especially nice are the plastic shoe racks. They keep shoes off the floor and can be moved readily for cleaning underneath them.

- Closets look neater if you use the same type of hanger for each item. Also, hang items of the same size together. Blouses and skirts at one end, dresses and gowns at the other.

- A good trick for necklaces and chains that tend to tangle together on your dresser is to install a wooden cup rack inside the closet. Hang your necklaces and chains and never have to untangle them again.

- Do give your clothes room to breathe. Your clothes should hang freely on the rods.

- Double top shelves are an excellent way to provide extra storage for seldom-used items.

Front or Hall Closet

Halls seem to be filled with coats, mittens, boots, etc. Where do you put them all? Purchase several stack-bins to put on a shelf in the closet. The stack-bins are good organizers for mittens, scarves and hats. Label each bin with a family member's name so each person can locate their belongings quickly.

Linen Closet

Did your mother have a great looking linen closet? Would you be embarrassed if your house guests accidentally opened your linen closet door? It's not hard or time consuming to keep it organized and neat. You just have to learn a few tricks of the trade. All towels, sheets, pillowcases and tablecloths should be folded neatly in a consistent manner, in the space allocated.

Paper Bag Pull-Ups

Toss closet discards into handled paper bags. Pick up two bags, one in each hand, that each weigh three to five pounds. With arms extended and slightly bent, lift them waist high. Repeat. Work up to twenty-five repetitions. Just think, the more you throw away, the better shape you'll be in!

If you have teenagers at home, and if they are anything like mine were, you probably wash an awfully big stack of towels. I truly think mine used one towel for their hair and one for each arm and leg and then one more just to make an even number. A good way to solve this problem is to buy each family member two large bath towels, each person getting their own color. Then, inform them that they are to keep the towel in their room— hung, not on the floor! — and that those towels are all they get for the week. Of course, you could simplify this by putting a combination lock on the linen closet door.

If your mother didn't display a great looking linen closet, it's because she didn't know how. But, follow these simple steps, and you will!

To Fold Towels:

Lay the towel flat on a table or counter. Fold it lengthwise into thirds, overlapping the edges in the center. Make the first long fold to a third of the way in. The second fold laps over, but not quite to the edge.

Fold each end toward the center, then fold it in half. Even towels with fraying edges will look great in the closet.

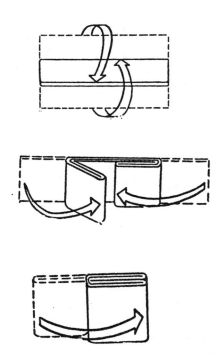

To Fold Washcloths:

Fold a washcloth lengthwise into thirds, overlapping edges in the center. Again, don't go quite to the outer edge on the last fold. Thirds first, then fold in half.

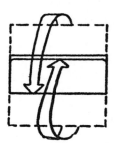 

To Fold Fitted Sheets:

Fitted sheets are a challenge to fold neatly. The secret is in the corner pockets—they all get nested into one pocket like spoons nesting in a drawer.

This works best if you have a large flat surface on which to work. First, fold the sheet lengthwise once by bringing the two longest edges together. Allow the corners at both ends to hang loose with the corner pockets right side out. Push both left hand pockets into each other. Do the same for the right hand corners. Fold the sheet end to end. All four corner pockets should now be in the same corner. Tuck the corners into each other.

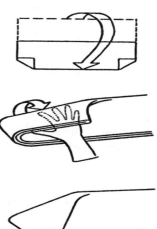

Take this slightly irregular, but now manageable shape, and even it off by folding into thirds. Fold in half from the other d i r e c t i o n and it should look tidy and square.

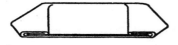

After folding linens, place them at the bottom of the appropriate stack. You'll rotate the linen, insuring uniform wear of the articles.

Don't throw away any old sheets that are 100% cotton. They make excellent cleaning cloths.

Broom Closets

Most people don't make the most of their broom closet space. Everything seems to collect on the floor.

- Construct a center divider and a couple of shelves. Put your vacuum cleaner and attachments on one side and broom, dust mop, etc. on the other. Install hooks or pegboard on the doors to hang the dustpan and whiskbroom.

- Store cleaning products on the top shelf on a turntable. They'll be out of reach for smaller children yet easy for you to find.

- Add a small set of plastic drawers or a caddy to hold screwdrivers, tape and other small items needed for quick repairs.

Making your closets work for you, instead of the other way around, is worth the effort.

And for heaven's sake, clean the door knobs to every closet door, and every other door, frequently. They are the most-often *touched* part of your house yet most people never think to clean them.

Laundry Room

Lots of people don't have a separate area in which to do their laundry. Some use their basements for this purpose. People throw their clothes down the stairs and have piles all over the place. The washer and dryer usually have at least an inch of dust on the top of them. Then, they dread going down to do the laundry.

You don't have to have a fancy place or a special room to do laundry in order to keep it looking nice. All that's needed is a little organization. Start by making sure you have proper lighting. You can't see what you're doing in the dark. And evening is when most working people do their laundry.

- Get an old table of some sort for folding your clothes.

- Put up a couple of clotheslines for hanging up clothes as soon as they come out of the dryer. Keep a supply of hangers on the line.

- Put up some large hooks—one for each family member. At our house, each has their own hook and designated pile on the table. When laundry was removed from the dryer, it was folded or hung according to name. Twice a week I sent out an order for everyone to take his or her laundry upstairs.

- Clean socks go into a container. Once a week it was the duty of my youngest child to mate them and put them away.

A few plants in the laundry room window add a nice touch, and the humidity does wonders for them.

- Hang cheery curtains. Keep all your clothes in a hamper or basket until you can get around to washing them. Sweeping or vacuuming the floor only takes a minute and it's worth the effort!

Above all, take the time to wipe your washer and dryer off once each week.

Chapter 8

Spit & Polish: Cleaning Various Surfaces

Betty and Dawn were scheduled to clean the upstairs duplex of a working client. The woman living downstairs was instructed to let them in. She wasn't home. After searching under the doormats and trying doors, they went to a gas station and called the office for further instructions.

We were there within minutes and discovered a balcony around back. We could see a door, which we assumed would let us into the upstairs apartment. Maybe, just maybe, the door would be unlocked.

A neighbor was watching from his backyard, so we asked him for a ladder. He gave us a suspicious look and declared he didn't have one. We made our own ladder with our hands and boosted Betty, the lightest, up to the balcony.

We were in luck. The door was open, and Betty was able to let us in to get the job done.

Why that neighbor didn't call the police is anybody's guess. Apparently, he tolerates breaking and entering as long as he doesn't have to supply any equipment.

Brass

Some brass polishes must be washed off thoroughly because they are acidic and can stain if left applied. Others however, may be wiped or rubbed off, because traces of polish won't stain. It's a good idea to restrict your choice to a wipe-off polish for objects that can't be submersed or rinsed.

Copper

Copper is used in many decorative items for the home. It can have a bright, shiny surface or a satin (burnished) luster. Copper darkens quickly with use, but plain air tarnishes it also—to a lesser degree.

Before cleaning, check to see if your copper item has a protective lacquer finish. If it does, don't use a cleaner or polish on it. Just wipe with a damp cloth and dry. After cleaning your copper with an acid-based cleaner, wash in warm soapsuds to help deter discoloration.

The Abs-olute Squeeze

Want a washboard flat stomach, but no time for sit-ups? The solution—put the squeeze on flab while you are polishing wood or metal. Stand with your knees positioned hip-width, contract abdominal muscles, hold for a full 10 seconds. Repeat 20 to 30 times. Each squeeze is as efficient as a full sit-up.

Silver

Too often, silver finds its way to the china cabinet to be displayed until it's distributed according to the final will and testament.

If you care for your silver properly (and use it), the older it gets, the better it looks. Be careful when polishing silver plate. Bearing down with the polishing rag in an overzealous manner could wear off some of the silver plate.

- Don't wear rubber gloves when polishing your silver. The rubber promotes tarnish.

- Dust your silver regularly and wash only with mild detergent. Use a soft toothbrush to clean intricate patterns in the silver.

The silver pieces you keep for decorative purposes are best kept shiny if lacquered by a jeweler. Then they'll never need polishing again!

Pewter

Pewter is a slightly soft metal that can have either a high polish finish or a soft satin sheen.

Pewter won't tarnish easily. Of course, if you want discoloration and stain, put pewter in a dishwasher. Otherwise, sink-wash pewter pieces in warm, not hot, water and a mild detergent. Dry promptly. Store pewter away from direct heat.

Flitz® does a fine job of polishing pewter and any metal though you may have to look in janitorial supply houses for it. Other products you could use are Brasso® or Wright's® products. Be sure to read the manufacturer's cautions before using them on any product.

Wood

When polishing wood furniture with an oil or wax, rub with the grain of the wood. Use a clean, soft cloth and rub until a clean fingerprint won't leave a mark on the finish.

Heat marks or water spots on furniture can be treated using the information on page 67.

Wall paneling can be oiled periodically by using a soft, clean applicator pad on a long handled mop.

The Great Salad Bowl Debate

Although many people swear you should never wash a wooden bowl, there's something to be said for the washing option. Oil dressings can and do turn rancid in time, and an unwashed bowl flavors future salads in a most unappetizing way. A quick, hot sudsy bath won't hurt the finish. Rinse and rub dry with a paper towel and get as much oil out as possible. Take a whiff; the bowl should smell like wood, not old grease. Rewash again quickly if necessary.

Coming Clean

Glass

To restore sparkle to glass vases, pitchers and decanters, place three tablespoons of uncooked rice in them. Then add a quarter-cup vinegar. Shake well and rinse. To remove odor and scum, add a little chlorine bleach to the washing solution.

Clean cut glass crevices with a damp cotton swab or a soft toothbrush.

Some glass gets cloudy from the etching effects of the minerals in your water (and each region has different water). Once etched, sadly, nothing brings them back.

Leather

To prevent leather furniture from drying out and cracking, rub it with castor oil or commercial leather conditioner about every six months. On light colored leather, be sure to use a light colored conditioner or white petroleum jelly.

Rubber Mats

When rubber tub or sink mats become mildewed and/or grimy, just toss them into the washing machine, along with a load of bleachable clothes or towels. The rubber comes clean and looks almost new. And no, don't run them through the dryer, please.

Try to make it second nature when purchasing anything to think about how you'll clean it and maintain it!

Water Softeners

If you live in a part of the country with hard water, buy a water softener. It'll be so much easier on your dishwasher, toilets and sinks. It keeps lime and iron deposits from forming.

Air Purifiers

If you can afford one, get an air purifier. It'll save you lots of dusting. We've worked in homes with air purifiers, and the furniture only needs dusting every other week.

Before your buy, however, check on the ease-of-cleaning of the air purifier. Most of them have filters that require periodic cleaning.

Humidifiers

Humidifiers can harbor potentially harmful bacteria. For that reason, your humidifier should be cleaned frequently. It's especially important to clean it if it's been sitting idle for awhile. The standing water becomes a breeding ground for bacteria that can become airborne and cause serious illness.

Your humidifier comes with specific cleaning instructions. But if you have misplaced them, follow these simple directions:

- As with any electric appliance, make sure it's unplugged. Then remove the water tank and wash with a solution of one quart water and two tablespoons of household bleach. Rinse well.

- To remove the lime deposits, soak with a solution of one quart water and a 1/2 cup vinegar. Again, rinse well.

- Most filters can be washed in the vinegar solution. Don't use detergent. Some types of humidifiers have special filters that must be replaced.

- Wipe all remaining parts with a soft cloth dipped in the bleach and water solution.

Dehumidifiers

If you can divert the water from the dehumidifier directly into a drain the maintenance is much easier. Place the hose over the drain, or just place the humidifier over the drain. If that's not possible, empty the water often.

- To clean a dehumidifier, remove the water tank. Wash it with hot water and detergent.

- Use a brush to scrub the interior, and rinse well.

- To remove the lime deposits use a solution of one quart of warm water with a 1/2 cup vinegar. If it's very stained, let the solution soak, then finish cleaning. Again, rinse well.

> If you add one tablespoon of household bleach to the tank after you clean it, it helps prevent mildew from forming.

- Finally, clean the inside coils with a small canister vacuum about once a month.

Chapter 9

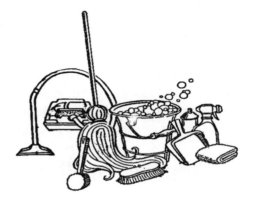

Gearing Up

When Domestic Engineering was newly founded, our clients provided the cleaning supplies and equipment. It didn't take us long to realize that people who don't do their own cleaning might not provide top-notch supplies.

One of our early clients supplied us with cleaning rags. She had carefully laundered them, folded them and left them with the other cleaning supplies. The first rag we unfolded was formerly an undershirt and was now a spidery web of jersey strands. The rest of the rags included two nylon socks, a tattered silk nightgown and a pair of panties. They were all in dreadful shape, even for rags.

Then we wondered, "What if this is laundry day?" Did we dare get furniture polish all over someone's favorite old panties? That very day we started supplying our own cleaning gear.

The fact that people need to save valuable time is obvious. You can forget all the commercials you've seen about little men cleaning your toilet bowls and genies coming out of bottles to give you a hand. It's time to be practical. Even though many products are packaged with real consumer appeal, they tend to be over-priced. Most won't do the job as well as the cleaners you can buy at a janitorial supply house or have on hand—baking soda, vinegar (which you can buy scented or scent your own) and bleach.

Cleaning Supplies

Look in your phone book, under 'Cleaning' or 'Janitorial Supplies,' to get your cleaning products. (Keep in mind that some janitorial supply houses only sell in bulk and only to professionals.) That's where companies like Domestic Engineering go to purchase their supplies. They often sell to individuals, too.

Years of experience have taught us that commercial products make easier work, and ounce-per-ounce, are less expensive. Professional supplies can also serve multiple duties and eliminate the need for many different types of cleaners.

People frequently ask what products I recommend for cleaning when not using professional supplies. The following list provides the basics. However, new products are coming out all the time. If you ask me the same question in a year, the list might change to include a better product.

- Porcelain and metal cleaner—a cleaner with some percentage of phosphoric acid: Cleans toilet bowls, tile, sinks, tubs and stainless steel. You still dilute it according to label directions. It does **not** harm skin, even when in direct contact. It has no dangerous vapors. Not found in your supermarket.

- Furniture polish—a good oil kind, such as lemon oil: Leaves wood looking like new.

- Degreaser—Removes the grease that's hard to clean from stoves. Formula 409® and Fantastik® are two good ones.

- Disinfectant cleaner—a must for kitchens and baths. Disinfectant and antibacterial cleaners are about the same. Try Mr. Clean® Antibacterial, Lysol® or Pine-sol®.

- Neutral cleaner—any good one: Use this to wash all floors because, as the name implies, the ph is neither alkaline nor acid. (Dish liquids, for example, are ph balanced.) It is neutral and does not leave a residue. It's especially good on hardwood floors. Damp Mop® is one I use. Also, Murphy® Oil Soap can be used to clean almost anything. It gets waxy buildup off furniture. And for one with a mild abrasive, there is *Clara's* Cleaning Scrub (see page 31) or Soft Scrub®.

- Carpet spot cleaner: Gone® works well. It contains no solvents that might soften carpet backing.

> Dilute purchased window cleaner with at least a cup of water. It needn't be as strong as packaged. You can also use diluted windshield washer fluid.

With these few products you can clean almost anything in your home. The important thing to remember about cleaning products is to give them time to do their jobs. Most people spray a cleaner on a surface, then wipe it right off. Give the product time. The next most common mistake is not rinsing a product off the surface. "Apply, rinse, dry," is the rule for most cleaning agents.

Coming Clean

Cleaning is an ongoing learning experience. Every day manufacturers come out with new materials and fabrics, which affect the way we clean. We are also faced with a seemingly endless list of supplies with which to clean. The best way to handle this is to always read and follow manufacturer's instructions. Cleaning is a learning—and rewarding—experience!

Cleaning Equipment

As with good products, good cleaning equipment can save hours of your precious time each month. Since you asked, I've come up with a list of my favorite cleaning supplies.

Basket (or pail): Get one with handles to store and carry cleaning supplies from one room to the next.

Bowl swabs: This is not a toilet brush, but a non-bristled, soft, absorbent cleaning tool. They're great for cleaning toilets, also for dusting blinds and lampshades. See page 113.

Brooms: You'll need a whiskbroom and a sweeping broom with plastic or natural bristles. A broom with angled bristles gets into corners the best.

Make your own tool for cleaning narrow spaces, such as between a range and cabinets. Glue (or tightly rubberband) strips of sponge to the bottom of a yardstick. Dampen with sudsy water and reach and clean formerly inaccessible places. Or rubber band or tape a paper towel tube or two to your vacuum hose. Collapse the bottom half of the tube to bend or fit into any small space.

Brushes: Scrub, wire, toilet and toothbrush. Buy cheap ones and replace them when they get too soiled or too ineffective to use. Use a scrub brush to clean grout in showers. A wire brush is used for oven grates and grills. A toothbrush, or small paintbrush, is to dust fragile objects and corners of furniture.

Cloths: Keep 100% cotton for drying, terrycloth for scrubbing and old flannel for dusting. You can't have too many rags. The new microfiber cloths work well, too.

Dusters: Buy lamb's wool dusters in various sizes. They're washable, and unlike feather dusters, don't readily fall apart.

Dustpan: Rubber is the best, with plastic as the next choice. Tin bends too easily. To keep dirt from sticking to your dustpan, coat it with a self-polishing wax.

Pails: Plastic ones are the lightest. A small ice-cream bucket does very nicely, too.

Pumice stone: Used to clean porcelain, it removes hard water stains and lime deposits. Can also clean grill and oven grates.

Mops: A yarn dust mop with washable head is great for dusting under places where a vacuum won't reach. Swiffer™ and similar products have easily changed heads, but don't do a great job with pet hair pick up.

Attach a small magnet to the top of a dust mop handle for a no-stoop pick up of pins, paper clips and other small metallic items.

Vacuum Cleaner: This piece of equipment is very important. Nearly everyday people use old vacuums hardly capable of running, let alone picking up dirt! You should buy the best you can afford. It's advisable to have two vacuum cleaners—an upright with a beater-bar for deep-down dirt removal, and a canister for draperies and furniture.

All About Vacuum Cleaners

Despite its "new plum color" or jet-age shape, the vacuum cleaner you buy has only one old-fashioned job to do—pick up dirt! Finding one that will do the job dependably and well is the challenge. Don't get stuck owning a first class vacuum cleaner that will suck up steel balls yet totally refuse to pick up a white thread on a dark rug.

Vacuum Two Step

Stand erect holding vacuum cleaner in right hand. Hold the left arm out to the side gracefully, like a dancer. Lunge forward on right foot, pushing vacuum in front of you. Return to original position, feet together. Move the body 30 degrees right and lunge again. Then lunge at a 90 degree angle to body. Change sides and repeat with the left side. Then move to another part of the floor and repeat the sequence. Thighs benefit from this exercise.

Technical information can tell you much about vacuums. However since many of us would be considered nontechnical, there is one sure way of measuring performance—observation!

Operate it yourself to assure that it'll meet your needs. If you can't get a home demonstration, get a demonstration in the store. Be sure the demonstration rug is similar to the carpets in your home.

Granular material such as sand or salt makes a good material to test for vacuum cleaner efficiency. Check the rug pile to see that the sand has been picked up, not pushed down.

Don't be influenced by tests such as these:

- Picking up filmy fiber or fine powder. Very little suction is necessary for this.

- Picking up a heavy object. Suction against a rug is your measure of cleaning efficiency.

- Using a new vacuum cleaner after use of your old cleaner on a section of rug. You would get an amount of dirt in your old cleaner's bag if the old cleaner were to be used again over the same section of rug. No cleaner gets all the dirt in just a few strokes.

Comfort, or ease-of-handling, is very important. Use it yourself and consider the effect on you after two or three rooms of vacuuming.

Noise of the vacuum is difficult to measure in the store, since a store's space and sound deadening factors (like clothes) would make the model seem quieter. Home demonstration is best.

Special features, such as full-bag indicators, automatic cord reel, varied height levels and a rainbow of colors may be available, but does the extra cost offset the convenience? Do the features add to the quality?

Coming Clean

A guarantee is offered with most vacuums. Buying from a reputable dealer is, in itself, a form of guarantee. However, read it and guard yourself against a possible void-of-guarantee, due to unauthorized replacement or repair. Some parts may be guaranteed for a shorter time than others. Also, check to see where the nearest service center is located. It may not pay if the nearest one is hundreds of miles away.

Kinds of Vacuum Cleaners

Vacuum cleaners for household use can be divided into three basic categories:

- Canister/Tank with Suction Only
- Upright and Agitation
- Combination Suction and Agitation

Water-filter vacuums are also available. Their sales pitch promotes unproven anti-allergenic qualities. They are a pain to use, heavy and clumsy, and do not work any better than any standard vacuum.

Bagless vacuum cleaners tout their ease of use. Maybe, but I like the idea of dirt going into a filtered bag that you can throw away.

Lightweight vacuums—not mentioning any names—that advertise extensively, are lightweight. They don't have the suctioning power of their heavier counterparts.

Canister/Tank

A motor-driven fan gives this model suction which pulls at the surface. The airflow carries dust and dirt into the dust bag.

This style vacuum offers:
- Best cleaning for general floor care,
- Best options for above the floor cleaning,
- And best at picking up surface litter and light, clinging dust.

A high degree of suction, plus a variety of attachments, make the canister a very versatile cleaner. The attachments are connected to the housing by means of a hose. The hose is flexible and usually reinforced with a spiral, wiry material. Attachments should be made of synthetic or noncorroding material. Most have removable or interchangeable brushes.

If you can afford only one vacuum, a canister should be your choice.

Upright

The cleaning ability of the upright comes from both agitation and suction. Suction pulls the carpet up against the brushes, or beater bars, which vibrate dirt and dust loose. The airflow then carries dirt into the dust bag.

The nozzle, or agitator opening, width should be about eleven inches. This width determines the time and energy you'll spend cleaning.

The head should adjust, manually or automatically, to various rug piles. The correct adjustment is crucial to proper rug cleaning. A bumper should surround the nozzle casing for furniture and wall protection.

Brushes should be thick and extend to both sides of the agitator. It's most practical to get a vacuum whose agitator has replaceable brushes, so an entire agitator replacement isn't ever necessary.

Beater bars are available, in addition to brushes, on some models. They'll supply beating action to the rug. Beater bars should be made of steel, not wood.

Attachments for the upright, for above-the-floor cleaning, are not as effective as the canister attachments, even in those with a two-speed motor. That's because the upright's power is used to drive the agitator. Attachments with the upright are also more cumbersome than those on a canister.

Combination

By taking a powered agitator and combining it with the powerful suction of a canister, manufacturers have come up with a tremendously effective vacuum cleaner. Highly recommended, nearly as effective and versatile as a canister.

> Never reach under a vacuum cleaner while the motor is on. If you suspect it is not running property, unplug the vacuum before tinkering around. The rule applies to all electrical or mechanical equipment.

If you want the dual approach to cleaning, you'll need both a canister/tank and upright or a combination. Check for comparative convenience, quality and cost.

Gearing Up

Care and Use of Your Vacuum

Like many household appliances, the vacuum often gets attention only when it isn't working properly. By knowing a few practical points about its care, you can avoid many problems. The owner's manual gives you detailed instructions about use and care that won't void the warranty. Build the following points into your cleaning routine.

Trouble Shooting

If the vacuum cleaner begins making a strange sound or the housing gets unduly warm or if there is a sudden drop in suction, turn the machine off and unplug it. It may be one of the following problems:

- Does the dust bag need changing or emptying?
- Are any of the air passages clogged?
- Is the agitator brush clogged with thread or hair?
- Is the belt broken or pulled off the motor pulley?

Remember that the greatest cleaning efficiency of the vacuum occurs when the nozzle is flush with the surface being cleaned. If angled upward or downward, the cleaning efficiency is diminished. That's why the nozzle should swivel, especially for under furniture. With an upright, you can hear the agitator against the rug if the nozzle is properly positioned.

A good vacuum, with a little maintenance, should last about as long as a good marriage.

Chapter 10

Clean Thinking: Remodeling or Building

Domestic Engineering once got a call asking if we would clean a houseboat. The owner, Stony, said he lived there year-round. So it sounded like any house cleaning job, with the possible addition of motion sickness.

Stony and I met at a dock, where I recognized him to be the bearded one in the company of two Rottweilers. He boarded us on a launch that ferried us to the houseboat. As my hair ruffled in the breeze, I pictured a luxurious boat outfitted with awnings and deck chairs, umbrellas and potted plants. Not that I truly thought Stony and his dogs lived on a yacht, but I needed to visit "my happy place" just then.

We got to the 'bump' in the seaweed Stony called home. He gave me a tour, and I kept an eye out for flotation devices. I imagined calling our insurance agent to report the untimely drowning of a cleaning lady. The impracticality of launching out to a job is what officially ruled out a client relationship. But off the record, "All shipwrecks don't sink," is the lesson I learned that day.

This information is for anyone who is building or remodeling a home. It can also be a valuable resource for people who rent.

We all like to make improvements in our living areas. And I hope this guide helps you make decisions that decrease your future housework.

Clean Thinking

It doesn't matter where you live—house, apartment or town home—you can make improvements that cut down on your cleaning time. The secret is to develop a cleaner's point of view. Simply put, before you buy or replace anything in your home, ask yourself "How will I clean it?" It may be cute and it may be fashionable, but is it cleanable?

Think about the cost of extra maintenance:

An extra:	...in a year, adds:
Five minutes, two times a day	61 hours
One half hour, two times a week	52 hours
Two hours a week	104 hours

Your home should contain only as much space as you really need. Focus your attention on creating a house that's large enough to accommodate your family's individual needs, but also one that doesn't have a lot of wasted space. Remember—the more space you have, the more area you must heat, air-condition and clean.

Coming Clean

Coming Clean

Windows and Doors

If you're determined to have Levolor® blinds in you home, vertical would be the best choice. They don't catch dust or grease and stay cleaner longer. Horizontals are a nightmare to clean. You might also think about getting the vertical blinds with the salt-and-pepper look. They hide a lot of dust.

Louvered doors can be put in the same category as Levolor® blinds. Those little slats collect dust quickly. They should be vacuumed once each week to keep them dust-free. Each louvered door adds at least five minutes a week to your cleaning time.

Floor-to-ceiling mirrors are a real nuisance to clean. The lower part attracts fingerprints. And the upper part requires using a stepstool or ladder every time!

Flooring

For carpet, nylon, hi-lo, earth-toned sculptured carpet is best. Lighter-colored carpeting shows dirt quickly, and colors show lint. Of the two evils, lint is easier to cope with.

When buying carpet for stairs, purchase an extra foot of carpeting. Have the carpet layer tuck the extra amount underneath, at the top and bottom of the stairs. When the carpet begins to show wear, have the carpet layer pull out the extra amount and move it up.

The stairs always show wear faster than any other area of a carpet. Change the point-of-wear to allow the steps carpet to last as long as the rest of the carpet. I've seen people replace all their carpet just because the stairways looked so bad.

Don't let anyone clean your carpets with shampoo that contains coconut oil. It attracts dirt!

The best choice of no-wax vinyl flooring would be a medium-colored floor. A light floor shows the dirt and a dark one shows all the dirty footprints. Stay away from floors with little grooves. The indentations collect dirt that must be removed with a scrub brush. Clean no-wax floors at least once a month. A nice multi-pattern tends to hide dirt and scratches.

No-wax floors are great! Get one with a high-gloss. It'll stay shinier longer.

Also, if a floor has cushion, it damages more readily than a non-cushioned floor.

Walls

Paint walls, or install wall treatments. But, if you have children or grandchildren, use low-gloss enamel paint (not flat), and/or purchase a good quality, washable vinyl wall covering. None of that elaborate wall covering or unfinished wood, if you want to keep your maintenance low. Paint lasts an average of three years. Wall covering lasts nine to ten years. So although wall covering costs more, it lasts almost three times longer. Buy the best wall covering or paint you can afford to save time and money in the long run.

Lighting

- Choose bathroom light fixtures with care. It's trendy for the mirror to be surrounded with clear bulbs. The light is excellent for applying makeup, but remember, each of those bulbs must be dusted and cleaned regularly. It's better to have something protecting the bulbs. (Hairspray seems to stick to everything in a bathroom.) A hanging light is good, but please, no clear globes! Clear globes can't be washed and replaced without leaving a few fingerprints.

- Kitchen light fixtures are needed in the ceiling and over the sink. They're exposed to a lot of grease, so they'll have to be cleaned often. A milk-white globe hides the most grease. Recessed lighting is better yet. The lights are protected from kitchen grease and dust.

- Bedrooms and living rooms don't require ceiling lights. To save cleaning time, use lamps only. Lamps provide soft lighting, direct or indirect, and should meet all needs.

- For hallways and entryways the most important lighting issue is location. Those little round globes hanging over your stairs look super until they get dirty. You can usually reach the first one to clean it properly, and if your arms are long enough, maybe even the second one. But look out for the third one! You wouldn't believe some of the contortions we've had to perform to wash hanging light fixtures. Be sure the lights can be reached with a stepstool or ladder. If you choose the brass and clear-glass type of fixture, check to see if the glass slips up and out, or if you have to take the fixture entirely apart.

- It's easy to dress up a dining room with a Waterford crystal chandelier. Who isn't drawn to all those beautiful prisms? Keep in mind how long it takes to clean one of them. Depending on the size, it can take from ninety minutes to two hours to clean a crystal chandelier properly. The best fixture for a cleanable dining room is one with removable glass chimneys.

With any light fixture, make sure the parts can be easily removed for cleaning.

Kitchen

- Don't leave a space between the ceiling and the cupboards. Most people display dust-collecting items in that space.

- Build your cupboards to the ceiling. It'll give you more storage space and less to clean.

- Stay away from grooves or protruding designs on the fronts of cupboards. They're real dust catchers. Anything that protrudes catches dirt.

- Don't paint cupboards white. Talk about work! Every smudge and drip shows.

- I know they're in fashion, but don't put glass fronts on cupboard doors. Not only will you have to keep things in the cupboards organized, but you'll have another surface to clean.

- Ornate handles on cupboard doors are more trouble than they're worth. Dirt and grease adhere to the handles and make them impossible to clean. Think of how many times the handles are used. Hands aren't always clean when opening cupboard doors. Smooth handles are best.

- Open shelves, instead of cupboards, are fine if you don't mind eating from dusty, grimy dishes. Seriously, forget open shelves if you can have closed cupboards.

- Marble counter tops are a lot of work to maintain. Acids, such as vinegar and harsh cleaning compounds, can stain them. If you can afford to spend lots on countertops, Corian® or granite work better.

- Ceramic tile countertops create their own headaches. Where there is tile, there is grout, and grout must be scrubbed with a brush.

- Wood (or butcher block) countertops aren't easy to maintain. They must be treated, and even then they'll look terrible in a short time.

- Don't get rough-surfaced countertops. Someone has to scrub with a brush to remove the dirt that settles in the low spots.

- Get the best grade stainless steel sink you can afford. Lower grade stainless steel doesn't wear as well.

- Don't be tempted to get a colored sink. They show scratches and lime deposits. Get the sink installed at least an inch from the backsplash. It allows room to clean behind the tap.

- A single tap faucet is all you need to dispense both hot and cold water. Less to break, less to clean.

- Refrigerators provide the exception to the smooth surface rule. A pebbled finish for a fridge hides the fingerprints.

- Don't spend the extra money for an indoor water dispenser for the refrigerator. Lime deposits build up. After a short time, that area will never look clean again.

- Forget stainless steel appliances. They look great when you first install them, but they're difficult to clean and maintain. If you burn something on the stove, it's hard not to scratch the surface while cleaning it up. And just try to remove tape from a stainless fridge!

- Say no to black appliances. It's the same cleaning nightmare as stainless. They show every mark. Buy appliances in white or almond. They won't go out of style, and they won't clash with any decor.

- Get a stove that vents to the outside. A downdraft, or circulating hood, doesn't do the same job of removing cooking odors and greasy air.

- Don't even think about glass tabletops. You can spend hours trying to remove spots and streaks. Half of them, remember, are underneath the table.

- Stone flooring is durable, but it is also hard to stand on for long. And, since stone feels hard, but is really a soft surface, washing causes it to chip and deteriorate.

Coming Clean

Bathroom

- Jacuzzi® owners I've known admit to seldom using them. They're difficult to clean. If you don't take long baths now, odds are you won't take long, jet-charged baths.

- Stay away from glass shower doors if you're not prepared to squeegee them every time you use them. There are many shower stalls on the market that don't need doors. Get creative with a great shower curtain. If you get tired of it, toss it.

- If you tile, use large tiles. The bigger the tile, the less grout area. Grout is tough to clean. Please don't set white grout.

- Marble looks good in a bath, but it water spots and stains with lime. There are attractive ceramics that look like marble and clean easily.

- Install a deep sink in the bathroom. It keeps water splashes to a minimum. And, it makes cleaning easier. Don't get any shape sink in the bath but round or oval. Odd shapes or grooves collect dirt. Keep liquid soap next to the sink rather than a bar of soap.

- Get a suspended toilet. If not suspended, at least get one that is molded into one piece.

- Don't get medicine cabinets with glass doors. They have tracks the doors slide on. Dirt and toothpaste get in the tracks and turn to cement.

- Keep the vanity mirror at least a few inches up from the countertop. It keeps some of the splashing down.

- Install a good ceiling fan, vented to the outside, to keep mildew to a minimum.

- Don't use wood in a bathroom except for doors, moldings and cabinet fronts. Water rots wood and eventually, no matter what it's coated with, it'll look bad.

Living Room

- Avoid tufted sofas and chairs. They're real lint catchers.

- Sofas and chairs with loose cushions create cleaning problems. The cushions are never in place, and children tend to remove the cushions and build forts with them—sound familiar?

- Sofa or chair cushions should have cording around the edges. Cording prolongs the life of the cushion and helps the cushion to hold its shape.

- Extremely dark or extremely light upholstery is going to show lint and dirt.

- Don't accumulate furniture with grooves and ornate moldings.

- Wicker and cane furniture are best avoided, as are elaborate lampshades. Remember, the flatter the surface, the quicker you dust. Even the new "wicker" furniture that advertises it can be hosed down, still has grooves and dents that collect dust.

- End tables or coffee tables with glass inserts are even worse to clean than glass-only tabletops. There are two different surfaces to clean, which requires two different cleaners.

- Bi-fold fireplace doors are almost uncleanable. The doors should open all the way for cleaning. That simple thing can save hours of frustration.

- Don't place lots of little throw rugs in traffic areas. Confine the dirt to a few larger rugs you can shake off the deck or outside.

- Some very nice picture frames are covered with black velvet on the back. Once they get dusty, it's very difficult to clean them.

Buy Right

Before you buy anything for your home, ask yourself these questions:

- Do I really need it?
- Where will I put it?
- Does it blend with other furnishings?

Asking yourself these three simple questions before buying could save you lots of money and garage sales.

Chapter 11

That Time of Your Life: Seasonal Chores

We have several customers who, for one reason or another, do not want their husbands to know they have cleaning help. One, "Ms. Procrastinator," discovered that her husband's relatives were coming for a visit. As usual, she was way behind in her cleaning. Realizing she could not possibly get everything done in time, she called Domestic Engineering to schedule cleaning for a day she was sure that her husband would be at work.

Our workers arrived and everything was going quite well until around 11 A.M., when whose car should she happen to see pulling in the driveway, but her husband's.

"Oh, no," she cried. But being the quick thinker she was—we have found that many people who work slow, think fast—she ushered her cleaners into the kitchen and poured each of them a cup of coffee. When her husband entered, she successfully convinced him they were new neighbors who just dropped by for a visit.

So, if you find yourself needing cleaning help and don't want your spouse to know, keep the coffee pot on!

Spring and Fall Cleaning

Domestic Engineering's alternative to a spring and fall cleaning is to clean two rooms thoroughly each month.

Set aside a certain day each month to do your thorough cleaning. Consider the cleaning "an appointment" that you cannot forget. Schedule a day in the first week of each month (any day that is convenient for you). That will make it easier to remember.

Since the kitchen and bathroom are mostly wet-cleaned, let's suppose this is a living room, and it needs an all-out cleaning.

*Spring and Fall—*Living Room Cleaning

Take down the curtains, draperies and shades. Fold them and move to another room. They can be washed or dry-cleaned later.

Wash windows on the inside, window frames and sills (screens also, if on the room-side of the windows). Use a glass cleaner solution on the glass and a Murphy® Oil Soap solution on the wood. Clean painted windowsills with a neutral cleaner.

Now that the windows are clean and you can see the rest of the dirt, plan your next moves carefully. Work from left to right and from top to bottom. If the walls need washing, call in the volunteers (willing or drafted) to help you move furniture out of the way. Turn back the rugs or cover the carpeting with a drop cloth.

Take down pictures, mirrors and bric-a-brac. Mix a pailful of wall cleaner solution. Gather several old terrycloth towels and a big sponge.

Start in one corner of the room and remove any dust and cobwebs with a dust mop or broom.

Dip your towel or sponge in the cleaning solution, squeeze until wet, but not dripping, and wash the wall, starting at the baseboard and working up toward the ceiling. (By washing down, any runny drips would leave "clean spots," which are hard to remove.)

Wash the wall with a side-to-side arm motion, doing about a three-foot-wide section, moving from left to right. If you can't do all four walls in one day, continue at least, until you reach a corner. Change the water as soon as it becomes dirty. If the walls are very dirty, repeat this procedure. Sometimes it's easier to paint.

Dry-clean bare wood floors with a wood floor cleaner containing wax. Apply it with a soft cloth or a long-handled lamb's wool applicator. A thin film is all that's necessary. It'll dry quickly with little need for polishing or buffing.

Step Stool Stomp

During your spring and fall cleaning get out the step stool for those hard to reach places. You can also firm up your fanny at the same time. Using the step stool, bring up your right foot, then left foot, to the same rung. Then step back down. Build up to 20 to 30 repetitions. No buts about it, this is a great exercise!

Shampoo carpet, if necessary. You may want professional carpet cleaners. They have the know-how and equipment to do the job properly.

Remove the contents of any open, painted shelves. Wash them with a wall-cleaning solution. Dry with a clean piece of terrycloth. Replace books, etc., only after shelves are thoroughly dry. Dust the books before returning them to the shelves.

Dust, then polish with your favorite furniture oil, all the wood furniture. Vacuum the upholstered furniture. Make a note to yourself if you see stains or spots. Don't clean them today.

Wipe off the curtain rods. Re-hang the cleaned curtains. Dust or wash decorative accessories, and clean any light fixtures. Wash mirrors, frames and glass for pictures, then re-hang. Dust lamp bases and shades. Wash the washable ones.

Stand back, or lie down, to admire your room. It should smell great and look sparkling clean!

The preceding cleaning information can be applied to any room in your home, except for the bath or kitchen. Procedures for them are somewhat different.

Spring and Fall—Bathroom Cleaning

One of the most important, and most-used, rooms in the house is the bathroom. Special attention should be paid to that area.

- Begin by removing and washing rugs.

- Wash window curtains and shower curtains.

- Wash windows, walls and woodwork.

- Clean tile and shower doors, including items on the wall.

- Clean closets and cabinets.

- Disinfect the tub, toilet and sink.

- Remove, then wash, all items on the counter.

- Wash counters and replace cleaned objects.
- Apply oil to any wooden holders to help protect the finish.
- Clean all light fixtures.
- Wash and disinfect floor.

Spring and Fall—Kitchen Cleaning

- Take down and wash the curtains.
- Clean the inside of and, weather permitting, outside of windows.
- Remove and wash all items on the walls.
- Wipe down walls and woodwork.
- Empty cupboards and drawers, and wash the interiors.
- Organize and replace items. Now is a good time to get rid of chipped dishes and the things you'll never use.
- Wipe down and oil the outside of wood cupboards, paying special attention to areas around handles.
- Clean interior and exterior of refrigerator, stove, microwave and dishwasher.
- Clean and polish all small appliances.
- Remove articles from countertops and wash them. (Stains on Formica® countertops can be removed with bleach).
- Clean table and chairs with a germicide. Pay special attention to legs and crevices.
- Scrub floor thoroughly and wax.

Periodic Cleanings

- Defrost refrigerator and freezer.
- Clean range and oven, burners and drip pans. Rinse cleaned areas with water and vinegar solution to neutralize any alkaline residue.
- Wash curtains, windows, and blinds, if necessary.
- Wash walls and woodwork, including the baseboards.
- Wash or dust light fixtures. (Make sure bulb is cold.)
- Clean the paneling and wash wallpaper, if necessary.
- Wash throw rugs, blankets, spreads, pillows and slipcovers.
- Shampoo large rugs and upholstered furniture.
- Organize and clean the closets and kitchen cabinets.
- Clean radiators, vents, range hoods and fans. (Oil when necessary.)
- Vacuum mattress, box spring, and frame. Wash mattress pad, and turn mattress as necessary.
- Polish silver, copper, brass and other metals.
- Wash and disinfect garbage and trash containers.
- Wax floors by hand or with a machine.
- Wash screens and storm windows.
- Wash shower curtains and glass doors.

And once a year, give yourself a break. Delegate or hire out chores for a week—or two, or three!

Mail Order Sources

The Queen's Store *Linda Cobb's* online store
Queen of Clean, PO Box 655, Peoria, AZ 85380
Palace Potty Puff (johnny mop)-item #103
$4.50 plus $3 p/h

Don Aslett's Cleaning Center
1-800-451-2402, call to order or call for free catalog
www.cleanreport.com
Bowel Caddy & Johnny Mop Set $6.50 plus $4 p/h
Johnny Mop alone $2.15 plus $4 p/h

Jeff Campbell's Clean Team Catalog
1-800-717-2532, call to order or for free catalog
www.thecleanteam.com

Home Trends catalog
1-800-810-2340, call for free catalog
www.hometrendscatalog.com

Web Sites Worth Exploring

The Soap and Detergent Association
www.cleaning101.com

All About Home by ServiceMaster
www.allabouthome.com

Linda Cobb/The Queen of Clean®
www.queenofclean.com

Don Aslett/Clean Report
www.cleanreport.com

Home Trends message board
www.justaskjane.org

Hints from Heloise
www.heloise.com

Haley's Cleaning Hints
www.haleyshints.com

Organized Home:
organize/declutter/simplify/clean
www.organizedhome.com

The Libman Company
www.mamalibman.com

Murphy® Oil Soap site
www.murphyoilsoap.com

Summary of
Lean 'n Clean
exercises

Index

index

Cleaning With Clara!
A seminar to simplify your life

Clara Klutz *(Schar Ward's alter ego)* HATES housework! Wailing out country ballads on the subject and looking like the scrub woman on the Carol Burnett show, Clara lets you in on the secrets that professional housecleaners have used for years!

The comedy team of Clara Klutz and her daughter, Debra Varin, will entertain and provide you with information that will save you time and money...and have you laughing at housework!

For more information contact Schar Ward. Her e-mail address is Scharletward@aol.com or visit her website: www.cleaningwithClara.com

or contact:
Domestic Engineering Inc.
toll-free 1- 888-414-5078

Household Help Books
from Book Peddlers

Coming Clean
Dirty Little Secrets from a Professional Housecleaner
by Schar Ward $9.95
120 pages, 6"x8"

Coming Clean   **book with 8" squeegee**
$12.95

Baking Soda
Over 500 Fabulous, Fun and Frugal Uses You Probably
Never Thought of
by Vicki Lansky $6.95
120 pages, 6"x7"

Another Use For...101 Common Household Items
by Vicki Lansky $8.95
160 pages, 6"x7"

The Bag Book
Over 500 Great Uses—and Reuses—for Paper, Plastic
and other Bags to Organize & Enhance Your Life
by Vicki Lansky $6.95
120 pages, 6"x7"

For a free catalog or to place an order, call 1-800-255-3379, or send
a check *(add $3.50 p/h for first book, and an additional $1.50 for each additional book)* to:

Book Peddlers
15245 Minnetonka Blvd • Minnetonka, MN 55345
952-912-0036 • fax 952-912-0105
www.bookpeddlers.com
www.practicalparenting.com
vlansky@bookpeddlers.com